THE CRIMINAL'S
SEARCH FOR GOD:
SOURCES

By
David H. Lukenbill

A Chulu Press Book

Chulu Press First Edition published 2012

IBSN-13 978-0-9791670-9-6
IBSN-10 0-9791670-9-4

Published by The Lampstand Foundation

www.lampstandfoundation.org

For all those criminals who
studied deep things
with me in prison.

For Marlene & Erika Always

The penitential criminal working to reform other criminals wisely spends the rest of his life atoning for the harm he has done during his criminal life; not because the world requires it, but because the eternal balance requires it, his immortal soul requires it, and God wishes it.

Contents

8

Preface

This is the seventh book in an annual book series that focus on issues connected to criminal reformation, which I have authored as part of the work of the Lampstand Foundation.

This book is a reflection on the collection of ideas within a group of books—sources—that played such a large role in the development of my thinking; initially to deepen my criminality, but eventually becoming the soil from which my transformation and conversion to Catholicism grew.

Most of my exploration of the ideas in these books occurred in prison or shortly after release and as such, they were works from which I drew ideas that largely supported and expanded the underlying narrative of the criminal/carceral world within which I lived, and are largely congruent with its driving ethos.

When I was in prison I read whatever books were available in the prison library or those I could get mailed in with my very limited budget.

Consequently, I was unable to exercise the great array of choices available outside prison and subsequently, a prisoner intellectually as well as physically.

Now having slowly discovered the wealth of the words in the world, and informed by Catholicism—through which I filter everything—I have discovered that it matters what you read and in the great work of criminal conversion and reformation, it helps to become familiar with their intellectual sources.

The common element of these source books is that they inspired a deep and critical reflection upon the ways of the world, with a particular focus on the social models and ideals criminals are told represent the world and to which they should aspire as part of their eventual rehabilitation. Professional criminals *know* that these models and ideals are misleading and that *they and their way of life* are closer to reality. Their perspective, which was once mine, is that criminals and the non-arrested (who are also criminals) who gain riches, fame, and power, share opposite faces of one self, but the criminal is true to self while the non-arrested is not.

I do not know the depth of sway these writings have in today's prisons, but suspect it is still considerable, for there are, living in the maximum security prisons of America—I met many such in the federal penitentiaries of Leavenworth and McNeil Island—men deep into their 70's and 80's still retaining the ferocity and physicality of men decades younger, and they remember and hold fast to the ideas that have long resonated within them and it is to them that younger criminals look to for benchmarks of criminal stature and worth.

This book can serve as a supplementary transformative tool by being used as a guide for other criminals seeking to restructure their lives, who are not yet prepared to enter into the study of Catholic works, because the ideas being fleshed out through them are ideas universal to many, in particular, criminals.

Much of this source literature comes from the 1940's to the 1970's, when the social adulation of the outsider, the outlaw, and the criminal came into full flower, and it was during the latter decade, that the carceral world was truly beginning to shape the criminal world.

Genet (1964) in full form in the capturing of that carceral world shaping, writes of the criminal/convict.

> Convicts' garb is striped pink and white. Though it
> was at my heart's bidding that I chose the universe

wherein I delight, I at least have the power of finding therein the many meanings I wish to find: *there is a close relationship between flowers and convicts.* The fragility and delicacy of the former are of the same nature as the brutal insensitivity of the latter. Should I have to portray a convict—or a criminal—I shall so bedeck him with flowers that, as he disappears beneath them, he will himself become a flower, a gigantic and new one. Toward what is known as evil, I lovingly pursued an adventure which led me to prison. Though they may not always be handsome, men doomed to evil possess the manly virtues. Of their own volition, or owing to an accident which has been chosen for them, they plunge lucidly and without complaining into a reproachful, ignominious element, like that into which love, if it is profound, hurls human beings...Repudiating the virtues of your world, criminals hopelessly agree to organize a forbidden universe. They agree to live in it. The air there is nauseating: they can breathe it. (pp. 9-10)

The world of the maximum security prison, once you have adapted and found your place within its social structure, is possessed of many deep virtues highly prized by criminals; first among them being that what one truly is, is known by all; and any attempts to present a personhood—interior or exterior—that is not truly yours is soon discovered, with consequences apt to be fatal.

This is a forging and refining quality also found in combat, and it is largely why the world of the prison has —over the past several decades—begun to play such a large and influential role in the world of the criminal.

What one is rather than what one presents himself to be is also at the heart of the Catholic Church and the congruence between what the Church has always presented herself to be with what she actually is—though one must examine closely and deeply the actual record—is strong and true.

This examination of the sources shaping one criminal's life and the review of the books playing the seminal role in the development of my intellectual life—their literary essence and transformative impact—is directed, as is all of my work, towards those men and women in prison or out, whose lives are shaped through their exposure to books and the ideas within which have the power to create transformed criminals, deep knowledge leaders, who not only have the academy to thank for their knowledge, but the city streets and the prison tiers, and who are able, through inclination, redemption, education, and skill, to become a grassroots organizational leader of an apostolate that can generate the transformation of other criminals, inside or outside of prison.

It is directed to penitential criminals who are Catholics or potential converts who, because of their stature and leadership in the criminal/carceral world, will have significant success and impact in the work of criminal transformation.

It is directed to those individuals who committed crimes for money—professional criminals—to whom crime was a way of life and prison time an occupational hazard.

It is directed to those professional criminals who have spent at least five years in a maximum security prison—the benchmark of professional criminality after arrest and conviction.

It is from these criminals that the leadership in the carceral world comes and it is from them that effective reentry leadership will also emerge.

Each distinct human population has a certain cohort from which effective leadership usually emerges and it is also so within the criminal world.

There are certain characteristics and criminal experiences that serve as the foundation of criminal world leadership and others that preclude someone from being perceived as a leader.

Criminal world leaders are not informers, do not commit crimes against children and women, nor allow themselves to be victimized by others in the maximum security prisons where they serve their time.

There are many people who have served time—in an honor farm, medical facility, or other minimum or medium security prison, who have developed and managed prisoner rehabilitation efforts—but their work has not sprung from their leadership within the carceral and criminal world, a leadership and status investing their work with the credibility and gravitas to become effective rehabilitative work on a national scale.

Intellectual life is widespread among professional criminals in prison and it is a pursuit they have the time to pursue. The oft noted comparison of prisons with monasteries—Skotnicki (2008) notes: "My own conclusion is that the prison as we know it in the West originated in the penitential practice of the early church and in primitive monastic communities." (p. 6)—is partially true; though the Divine Office as practiced by monks and nuns is replaced by the Moloch game of acquiring and sustaining power and privilege from ever newly arriving contenders.

The intellectual life is, as D'Arcy (1954) writes in his life of St. Thomas Aquinas, the path to love.

> This distinction [between Kant & himself on the human intellect] brings out the second characteristic of the philosophy of St. Thomas. It is conspicuously a system compact and all-embracing, and the masonry has the hard white quality of reason. In contrast with friends, like St. Bonaventure, for instance, and many another

philosopher, he relies so far as is possible on reason and reason alone....

Love, if it be of a true quality, is begotten by knowledge. Knowledge makes for intimacy, and its supreme ardour is contemplation. Perfection, therefore, is to be sought in the intellect and not in desire; the latter presupposes that one has not yet the beloved object in a close embrace; possession belongs to the intellect, rejoicing that it is one with the other for whom the soul has longed. (pp. 44-45)

St. Thomas Aquinas (1948) teaches us that the intellect is a power of the soul, think upon that...

I answer that, In accordance with what has been already shown (Q. 54, A. 3; Q. 77, A. 1) it is necessary to say that the intellect is a power of the soul. For then alone the essence of that which operates is the immediate principle of operation, when operation itself is its being; for as power is to operation as its act, so is the essence to being. But in God alone His action of understanding is His very Being. Wherefore in God alone is His intellect His essence; while in other intellectual creatures, the intellect is a power. (*Summa Theologica* Q. 79, A. 1)

I could not have come to an appreciation of Aquinas without the early tutoring through the works examined in these pages, for it is through the critical search through the chaos of the thought of the world, that the "hard white quality of reason" of the thought of the Angelic Doctor will later come to resonate as the true sign of contradiction truth alone holds when stood up against the world.

This book is directed towards those criminals who become part of the long and winding path to the communal community of the Catholic Church—triumphant, suffering, militant—no matter at what place along that path they may be, for if they are on that path and if transformed criminals are close to them, then conversion is certain when they make the intellectual choice to transform themselves, to create from within a different person than what they were previously, a person whose motivation is based on the fullness of eternal truth, found only in the Catholic Church, the City of God, rather than on the transitory truth of the world, the city of man, the city of the prison.

Virtually everything of the world acts to validate the illusion that objective truth does not exist, but truth is so powerful that it always speaks to us. Even from the works of the illusionists—from whom many of the sources herein described come—the embedded ideas of truth call out to us, but we need the eye and mind of the Church to see the truth, for in it truth has been deposited since the beginning, first with the Jews and after Christ, with everyone willing to see.

I am speaking here of the Church through eternal time, the mighty ark of Christ guiding us, the pillar of fire leading through the desert to the land of milk and honey.

We must not become attached to the small and worldly Church, to the errant priests, nuns, and popes, for these shall always infect the People of God on earth, as they have throughout history and as is becoming increasingly evident, virtually conquering the institutional Church during the 20th Century, which the struggles of the 21st to reclaim her remain to be accomplished, but not in doubt.

Within the first universal catechism of the Catholic Church, that of Pope Pius V (1982) first published in the Year of Our Lord 1566, it is written:

> We are, therefore, bound to believe that there is one Holy Catholic Church. With regard to the Three Persons of the Holy Trinity, the Father, the Son, and the Holy Ghost, we not only believe them, but also believe *in* them. But here we make use of a

different form of expression, professing to believe the holy, not *in* the holy Catholic Church. By this difference of expression we distinguish God, the author of all things, from His works, and acknowledge that all the exalted benefits bestowed on the Church are due to God's bounty. (p. 113)

And men, even Peter, who lied thrice about our Lord and ran rather than keeping watch over the crucifixion with the Apostle John, and the three Marys, often betray God; though Peter, after Pentecost, became the rock our Lord proclaimed and died a true martyr's death, refusing to be crucified upright as Our Lord, but died hanging upside down on his cross.

The Holy Catholic Church was deeply infiltrated early in the 20th Century and redirected during the mid-century council, Vatican II.

One of the clearest signs of her misdirection—along with removal of the Latin Mass—was the scandal of ignoring the charge from Our Lady of Fatima.

The appearance of the Holy Virgin Mother to the three children, delivering the instruction for the Pope and all of the bishops of the world, to consecrate Russia, was ignored.

Consequently Russia became the single largest sponsor of the evil of communism in the world responsible for taking hundreds of millions of lives, and degrading billions more.

Even with that, the current time is the best of times—for it embodies all that has gone before—and it is the worst of times—as it embodies all that has gone before.

Laying blame, while a worthwhile intellectual exercise building a historic foundation upon which informed belief can rest, resolves little for it is as it is.

Peter is the embodiment of popes throughout history as dogma is embodiment of beliefs throughout history.

Everything that has happened in the Church is for the best.

The sexual abuse crisis revealed the true nature of the desanctification of the religious predators.

Vatican II's impact on liturgy led to Latin Mass redoubts where true Catholics live.

The legalization of abortion reveals the true nature of the world under its satanic prince.

We attach ourselves to the eternal truth of the Church—we love God, we love people, we protect the innocent, we fight evil—and every day, every minute, increase our knowledge of the truth, for it is the only path to eternal life.

We have the Lord to guide us and we have great teachers to teach us—St. Thomas Aquinas being supreme among them—and his work illuminates the great truth upon the narrow road to eternity, an eternity the Angelic Doctor entered just at that moment when he realized how little his words meant when compared to the beatific vision; but which mean so much to those of us reaching for that vision.

Finally, one of the most difficult chores in writing about the criminal/carceral world as a former criminal/prisoner is the misconceptions of many readers developed by the normative universe of criminal/carceral world books by former criminals/prisoners.

They tend to fall into two basic patterns: the penitential and the sociological and I have tried to keep each—as much as possible—from my books.

In order to help convince non-criminal/carceral world readers of the accuracy of my representation of my former world, I eagerly grab collaborating sources, for instance, the validating of one of our guiding criminal justice principles that precludes working with informants, pedophiles, or rapists because they do not have the criminal/carceral world status to become effective Catholic evangelizers—which is our essential mission; validation we found most clearly stated by Schiller (2012) in an article about the screening procedures one of the seminal prison gangs utilizes for membership:

> While the gang - which was born in the Texas prison system in the 1980s and operates statewide - tolerates drug dealers, killers and kidnappers among its ruffian ranks, there is no room for child molesters or rapists, officials say...
>
> Gang leaders also want to root out snitches by checking to see if a convict has done a respectable amount of time for his crimes. If he was cut loose too easy, it's a red flag signaling he might be a government informant. (n.p.)

Introduction

Rehabilitation and reentry are terms used by most rehabilitative practitioners to describe the process more accurately called criminal transformation. Rehabilitation or reentry are not proper concepts to use as they imply a return to something—a state of internality—that previously existed or in some community in which one previously resided, whereas professional criminals are generally born into the criminal world, and that is the only internality and community reality congruent with their perspective. Working from a rehabilitative or reentry perspective, as does the normative rehabilitative practitioner, sets the criminal transformation process on the incorrect intellectual setting, partly the reason for its continued failure, widely evident when the rehabilitation programs used by them are evaluated rigorously.

Rehabilitative/reentry practitioners generally define success or failure after a three year period post-release from custody when about 70% of criminals in the United States recidivate, including those released from several criminal justice sanctions— probation, parole, jail, or prison—but in our work through the Lampstand Foundation, we use it in reference to professional criminals released from a maximum security prison or a transitional facility after serving the bulk of their time in maximum security.

We use a ten year period of reentry as a benchmark of transformation as it allows for the fuller development of transformative behavior—and a more accurate reflection of return statistics— than the relatively short three year period does.

We believe that only transformed married Catholic criminals should be involved in developing and managing criminal transformation programs because Catholicism is the only truth potent enough to trump the truth of the world—informing the truth of the criminal world—and professional criminals who've served at least five years in a maximum security prison, possess a graduate degree, and a deep knowledge of Catholic social teaching, are the only ones who understand the carceral and criminal world well enough to present that truth with enough vigor and standing to influence personal conversions that will ultimately reduce recidivism.

It is only within the Catholic Magisterium that the robust story of Christ exists in its fullness with the power to destroy the lie told by the prince of this world, the foundation the truth of the world and the truth of the criminal world is built upon.

While the response to the crimes criminals commit in the world belongs to Caesar's police, courts, and prisons, the response to the individual human being who is the criminal—his transformation and redemption—belongs to God and the teachings of His Church.

The catechesis of the criminal brought through study of the history of the Church and her social teaching—Catholic doctrine presented in universal terms—will work. For within the social teaching will be found the unbroken line of truth connecting the transforming criminal to the beginning of creation and the institution in which truth exists, which has held to it for over two thousand years; something that can be said of no other institution on earth.

Christ specifically speaks to the criminal world who has been deceived into believing the truth of the world and living by the rules of men in the city of men, which the criminal does more boldly than the rest.

Being able to speak from brotherly love and deep knowledge, the transformed criminal, who once relished many aspects of his former criminal life, knows the failure of active love in the oft quoted "love the sinner, hate the sin" in a life where identification with the sin is often deep.

The Church dwells in the interior of man—in the communion with Christ—not in the community of men, and through its interiority guides the walking of the talking.

For centuries the criminal, like Cain, could be banished, or voluntarily disappear and begin life again as a new person, but no more.

Now all are connected and all crimes rest on the all-knowing digital conscience of the world and the only rebirth, even since ancient times, is through baptism.

Reaching this point within that leads to the path of transformation, requires long and consistent study which will result in the creation of deep knowledge, and the classic works which are already alive within the carceral world's library are those works reviewed in this book will be of great help in the development and exercise of that love of knowledge which can eventually lead to love of the teaching and history of the Church, resulting in conversion and transformation.

Criminal as Poet

Poetry is a powerfully attractive way for criminals in prison to express their inner life and its structured or free form, brevity, and spiritual roots, lend itself as an effective way to express suffering within a socially acceptable method with long history within the criminal/carceral world.

Outlaw poets share a certain aberrancy fully immersing them in convention bending reality reminiscent of criminal world values, but strangely apart from them also.

Three major poets—Ginsberg, Khayyam, Baudelaire—whose work illuminates the foundational ideas underlying the type of life often connected with criminality, infusing them with a sense of passion, destiny, and romantic foreboding within which criminals often sense a relationship and congruency that calls for a deeper exploration into many related works.

Many criminals, during the first reading of Ginsberg's poem *Howl*, begin such an exploration.

I remember when I first saw this poem, during my time in the Federal Correctional Institution at Inglewood, Colorado or as we affectionately called it "Little Alcatraz" due to its double barbed wire fence and multiple gun towers, making it somewhat impervious to escape.

This saddened me as I had escaped from my last three institutional confinements, Reno City Jail, Nevada State Foster Home, and Nevada State Reformatory and had planned to do the same here, but I was beginning to realize that I might be housed in a prison from which I could not easily escape.

Howl was smuggled into the prison as a handful of mimeographed sheets which was passed around to the group I hung out with, completely blowing our minds.

We didn't really read it too close, being too young (15-17) to have the more adult literary ability we would later grow into, but we latched onto the sense of freedom and artistry that seemed to be describing the kind of lives we lived, at least before our imprisonment.

Having developed a sense of alienation from the daily life of normality through a love of the criminal life that led them to prison, many criminals eagerly feast on this work, which not only validates their sense of alienation, investing it with a mythical penetration of the invisible secrets underlying the visible, while reshaping the ongoing narrative of the truth of the world, while putting it into a context that elevates rather than denigrates the criminal life.

From Ginsberg's (1956) first line:

> I saw the best minds of my generation destroyed by madness, starving hysterical naked,
> dragging themselves through the negro streets at dawn looking for an angry fix,
> angelheaded hipsters burning for the ancient heavenly connection to the starry dynamo in the machinery of night, (p. 9)

many criminals are hooked—I feel a thrill still reading these—and see the possibility of not just a senseless battering against the unthinking stone and steel prison which has resulted from their acts, but an actual artistic and beautiful life being created from the *apparent* chaos others see, though perceived by the criminal as the way life is supposed to be.

We can see in the Moloch verses of *Howl*:

Moloch the incomprehensible prison! Moloch the crossbone soulless jailhouse and Congress of sorrows! Moloch whose buildings are judgment! Moloch the vast stone of war! Moloch the stunned government!" (*Ibid*. p. 21)

a path to sacrificial understanding that illuminates a prison driven life.

In seeking out the real worship of the great god Moloch, which I later did, we find that he was a Carthaginian deity built of metal upon whose outstretched arms were cast the children of Carthage in a sacrifice dramatized by Flaubert (2007):

Every time that a child was placed in them [his arms] the priests of Moloch spread out their hands upon him to burden him with the crimes of the people, vociferating: "They are not men but oxen!" and the multitude round about repeated: "Oxen! oxen!" The devout exclaimed: "Lord! eat!"...

Nevertheless, the appetite of the god was not appeased. He ever wished for more. In order to furnish him with a larger supply, the victims were piled up on his hands with a big chain above them which kept them in their place. Some devout persons had at the beginning wished to count them, to see whether their number corresponded with the days of the solar year; but others were brought, and it was impossible to distinguish them in the giddy motion of the horrible arms. This lasted for a long, indefinite time until the evening. Then the partitions inside assumed a darker glow, and burning flesh could be seen. Some even believed that they could descry hair, limbs, and whole bodies. (Chapter XIII)

Moloch was a powerful image to present as representative of the culture in which we lived and attributes fitting its dark visage were readily apparent to the drug illuminated minds of those who resonated with the images so skillfully woven by the Beat poets.

Howl overturned every convention of its time and did so gloriously, artistically, and poetically; claiming, as cultural revolutionaries always do, that theirs was a better—a higher—way.

Howl and the other works of the Beats paid homage to outlawry and social chaos, a deep and long-burning fuel for the emergent criminal mind, reshaping and deepening the truth of the world in its slow trajectory towards full embrace of criminal world truth, and I raced with it.

The story of Omar Khayyam, the author of the *Rubaiyat,* is intriguing and has deep connections to criminal world culture, involving the birth of the assassins (one of Omar's classmates with whom a life- long pact was formed among three of them to help one another if any of them became successful, was the man who began the cult of the assassins and became the *Old Man of the Mountain,* a legendary outlaw of the Middle East) and the joy of living a life of sensuality as Khayyam (2007) says:

> Some for the Glories of This World; and some
> Sigh for the Prophet's Paradise to come;
> Ah, take the Cash, and let the Credit go,
> Nor heed the rumble of a distant Drum!"
> (Stanza XII)

The work has such beauty and so well presents the life of ease, drink, and pleasure for self that one is hard pressed to resist it when in that peculiar place of seeking answers to what the reality of prison and life in the criminal world are revealing.

So many of the treatises proclaiming the truths of the world wind up to be empty shells of words and ring sad, forlorn, or angry in a boldly defying acceptance—music to criminal ears—such as *Howl* or the melancholic quietness of Eliot's *The Hollow Men* (1980):

> We are the hollow men
> We are the stuffed men
> Leaning together
> Headpiece filled with straw. Alas! (p. 56)

Khayyam however, is joyful, worldly and one would think a wonderful drinking companion, a wise voice in the prison cell reminding criminals of the transient nature of life, the treasures yet to be discovered and the readiness to bend to the fate of the world which claims us all.

The narrative companion to *Howl* is centered around a road trip the author of *On the Road*, Jack Kerouac, takes with Neal Cassady, the criminal and former prisoner who was so much of a lodestar to three of the founding Beats: Ginsberg, Kerouac, and Burroughs.

His reality may be more important to the formation of the spiritual and literary roots of the Beats and Hippies—he was also the bus driver of the bus *Further* which Ken Kesey and the Merry Pranksters moved into legend chronicled by Thomas Wolfe in the *Electric Kool-Aid Acid Test*—than any of the writers whose poems and prose captured and preserved the journey of convention rebellion and the spiritual seeking way of life over the hazy decades.

Cassady was Dean Moriarty in *On the Road* and the gravitas of his place in Kerouac's thinking is evident throughout, as Kerouac (1999) begins in the first three sentences:

> I first met Dean not long after my wife and I split up. I had just gotten over a serious illness that I won't bother to talk about, except that it had something to do with the miserably weary split-up and my feeling that everything was dead. With the

coming of Dean Moriarty began the part of my life
you could call my life on the road. (p. 1)

In the middle of the book Kerouac hears from
Cassady/Moriarty, the secret of Cassady's vision, a vision
Kerouac desperately wishes to possess:

> Furthermore we know America, we're at home; I
> can go anywhere in America and get what I want
> because it's the same in every corner, I know the
> people, I know what they do. We give and take and
> go in the incredibly complicated sweetness
> zigzagging every side." (*Ibid.* p. 112)

Being able to be dropped down into any place in the
country, stone cold broke and without a friend—as one is
usually released from prison—and survive, even prosper,
within hours, is the mark of a professional criminal, a mark
I had met many times, and it is the knowing
Cassady/Moriarty possesses and Kerouac desperately
desires.

Kerouac ends *On the Road* paying homage to the one who
knows:

> So, in America, when the sun goes down and I sit
> on the old broken-down river pier watching the
> long, long skies over New Jersey and sense all that
> raw land that rolls in one unbelievable huge bulge
> over to the West Coast, and all that road going, all
> the people dreaming in the immensity of it, and in
> Iowa I know by now the children must be crying in
> the land where they let the children cry, and tonight
> the stars'll be out, and don't you know that God is
> Pooh Bear? The evening star must be drooping and
> shedding her sparkler dims on the prairie which is
> just before the coming of complete night that
> blesses the earth, darkens all rivers, cups the peaks
> and folds the final shore in, and nobody, nobody
> knows what's going to happen to anybody beside

the forlorn rags of growing old, I think of Dean Moriarty, I even think of Old Dean Moriarty, the father we never found, I think of Dean Moriarty." (*Ibid*. p. 293)

Neal Cassady/Dean Moriarty was the man who knows, the criminal poet from the criminal world, the one who was not only not afraid, but absolutely relished the deep night of city streets and unknown highways and starless views; and he shared his knowing with those who needed to know and a way of life was formed, within which the poetry of the criminal world deepened still.

On the Road begins and ends idolizing the criminal who can live freely, who sees deeply the reality below the convention the Beats are so earnestly rebelling against, becoming in actuality their new father, even giving them expression as the style of Cassady's famous letter to Joan Anderson becomes Kerouac's writing style.

Charters (1992) writes about the November 1948 conversation between one of the Beat founding writers John Clellon Holmes and Jack Kerouac, trying to define the new knowing being revealed and written about:

> He [Holmes] felt Kerouac's stories "seemed to be describing a new sort of stance toward reality, behind which a new sort of consciousness lay." Holmes responded to the "restless exuberance, the quality of search" that he senses in Kerouac's descriptions, and he urges Jack to characterize the new attitude by trying to define it in a phrase or two.

> As Holmes recalled the conversation, Kerouac replied, "It's a kind of furtiveness...like we were a generation of furtives. You know, with an inner knowledge there's no use flaunting on that level, the level of the "public," a kind of beatness—I mean, being right down to it, to ourselves, because we all

really know where we are—and a weariness with all the forms, all the conventions of the world....so I guess you might say we're a *beat* generation,' and he laughed a conspiratorial, the Shadow-knows kind of laugh at his own words and at the look on my face." (p. xix-xx)

His own words, but Cassady's—the criminal world's— reality, and ultimately Kerouac realized he had failed in his search and that worldly fame obscured rather than illuminated the eternal he really sought, just as drugs, sex, convention warping, and the following of whim and passion wrapped Cassady, Ginsberg, Burroughs and the others so tightly as to make them scream with existential pain they passed to us, passing still, priests and priestesses of nothing eternal, nothing real, all wrapped in candy colored flakes blowing in the wind.

Charters writes:

> His [Kerouac] decision to become a writer was encouraged by Allen Ginsberg, Lucien Carr, and William Burroughs, but in the auto-biographical novel *Vanity of Duluoz* (1968), which Kerouac wrote late in life about the period 1939-1946, he expressed reservations about his friend's wild behavior. In describing their association with criminals and drug dealers, and his own Benzedrine and alcohol addictions, he acknowledged that this "clique was the most evil and intelligent buncha bastards and shits in America but has to admire in my admiring youth." (*Ibid* p. 8)

As the end approached and as death parted them from the reality they thought they had discovered the secret of—but really only an escape from—a narrative, poetic, and song writing escape which writhed in anguish and self mortification based on no great vision of God, they finally realized the truth.

Kerouac was a cradle Catholic whose life and end was particularly and poetically tragic, as Cavanaugh (2012) writes.

> Kerouac's energetic narratives were uniquely suited to the changing cultural atmosphere in the U.S. Countless middle-class youths were turning against the expected way of life, with its "square" emphasis on responsibility and limits. With a narrative filled with drug use, casual sex, and ardent wanderings, *On the Road* was prime for real-life adoption by an army of young adults...

> As the author of this phenomena, Kerouac was a hero to these children of excess. But little did they know that the creator of their beloved text harbored political views and religious beliefs that were far different from, perhaps diametrically opposed, to their own. Their icon was, in fact, a Republican and a friend of right-wing stalwart William F. Buckley. And though he dabbled in Buddhism, Kerouac was essentially a lifelong Catholic who, at the apex of the counterculture movement, proclaimed, "Listen, my politics haven't changed, and I haven't changed! I'm solidly behind Bill Buckley, if you want to know."

> Kerouac was one hip scribe who could tell *Playboy*: "I am not ashamed to wear the crucifix of my Lord. It is because I am Beat, that is, I believe in beatitude and that God so loved the world that he gave his own begotten son to it."...

> Another problem with these beatnik ties was that, almost everywhere Kerouac went, others were expecting him to cut a rambunctious figure. A rather severe alcohol problem ensued, and his mental health began to deteriorate....

On the brink of despair, Kerouac launched a one-man retreat into the Big Sur mountains, along the central California coast. He was hoping that this solitary trek would curb his addiction and revitalize his creativity. Neither goal was accomplished; he was soon observed staggering drunk on the streets of San Francisco.

In the wake of this relapse, the *On the Road* legend headed back to his mother, for life as it once was. But there would be no surfeit of joy in Kerouac's last years. He was a disillusioned and resigned alcoholic, eventually succumbing to an esophageal hemorrhage at the young age of 47. Kerouac's funeral Mass was held in his hometown of Lowell, at St. Jean Baptiste Catholic Church, where he had served as an altar boy. (pp. 36-37)

There are other poems exerting a powerful pull on the sensibilities of criminals in prison—during the period when the carceral world began reshaping that of the criminal world—whether exploring the mysteries of the love between a man and a woman, perhaps wrapped in a deep allegorical mist, as many feel the poems of Walter Benton to be.

Walter Benton graduated from Ohio University, worked as a social investigator in New York, and served in the army during the Second World War, becoming a captain.

Benton's (1968) *This My Beloved,* his first published book of poetry—in 1943—and his most well known work, is a diary in verse and its opening line reveals the power of a mature poet:

> Because hate is legislated...written into
> The primer and the testament,
> Shot into our blood and brain like vaccine or
> vitamins." (p. 3)

The poetry embraced by the American carceral and criminal world, during whatever period of time, will relate those aspects of the criminal life emblematic of the reality seen by the criminal and the poetry of Benton does, in its foreboding and elegiac capturing of the emotional life between a couple or their loss.

Benton's (1960) *Never a Greater* Need, first published in 1948, was his selection of the best poems he wrote after the publication of *This My Beloved* and he had become famous.

Its closing lines reveal the growth of his poetic vision.

> I fail where you fail, seek what you would find...question
> What you would have answered—
> O will we ever know our rumored greatness
>
> who kill as stonemen killed for one's tongue or color,
> conscience or face of God,
> with piety on our lips and science shining in our eyes—
> embracing logic or the cross as an adulteress her husband." (p. 62)

Hunched over in dark cells these words were often read metaphorically, seen to represent the addiction driven world—the heroin addicts I met in prison loved Benton's work and they said he was also a junkie—the surcease from a pain seeking world, the world of self medication, the world criminals so often travel in, where many choose to dwell forever.

Two great poems from the criminal life are *The Blue Velvet Band* and *Stagger Lee*, both capturing in their own unique way a certain reality of the criminal world—the often ambiguous relationship between men and women and the honor-bound actions of the criminal often appearing incomprehensible to outsiders—and both poems loved by criminals throughout the country for many generations.

There are many versions of *The Blue Velvet Band*, but the one that rings closest to that loved by most prisoners is the version sung by Porter Wagoner (2007) which opens so hopefully romantic:

> One evening while out for a ramble the hour was just about nine I met a young maiden in Frisco at the corner of Geary and Pine.

And closes in prison, sent there by the girl with the beautiful hair, wrapped in the blue velvet band:

> They sent me to San Quentin for stealing Lord knows I'm an innocent man while the guilty one's somewhere a laughing and dancing the girl in the blue velvet band.

Stagger Lee also opens on a corner in the criminal city, at night, when the criminal world comes out and the lights shine so brightly, hiding the deep shadows looming, darkly inviting.

This work of poem and song, which has been so prominent in the criminal world, has been found to have originated from an actual event—which is surely also true, though as yet unsubstantiated, for *The Blue Velvet Band*—from the life of Lee Shelton, sometimes known as *Stagger Lee,* a criminal who murdered William Lyons on Christmas Eve in 1895 in St. Louis, and himself died in prison in 1912.

The traditional version by Lloyd Price (1959) opens:

> The night was clear, and the moon was yellow
> And the leaves came tumblin' down. . .
> I was standing on a corner
> When I heard my bull dog bark
> He was barking at the two men

33

Who were gambling in the dark
It was Stagger Lee and Billy
Two men who gambled late.

These poems, like many others which spoke to the life
conditions of the criminal and carceral world, circulated,
were refined and personalized by generations of criminals
to express their feelings about what they were
experiencing.

The long European tradition of singing praise of the
corrupt and criminal life—Petronius' *Satryicon*, Marquis
De Sade's *Justine*, Oscar Wilde's *The Picture of Dorian
Gray*, Thomas De Quincey's *Confessions of an English
Opium Eater*—seemed to be gathered together in a great
chest and wrapped in a gaudy bow through the work of
Charles Baudelaire (1991) and his aptly named major work,
Flowers of Evil in which he captures the essence of his
thought:

> The evil-minded poet, foe of the family,
> Darling of the devil and the homeless whores,
> Is welcome at both tomb and brothel, there to see
> His alcove with a bed that never knows remorse.

> (111 Two Good Sisters, stanza 2, p. 221)

All the criminal positions are here stated, the mental
stance and guiding principle, the freedom from family and
work-a-day entanglements, rightly fought against and
enemized; the love of the true patron, and the always
present playmates, from whose embrace time has no sting,
nor are there any remembrances of things as they might
have been.

Anna Balakian, in her Introduction to *Flowers of Evil &
Paris Spleen* captures as well Baudelaire's drive:

> One aspect of his turmoil, and a very important
> one, may not be as easily understood by current

readers; his struggle between Catholicism and agnosticism, an immense rebellion against both God and the devil. (*Ibid.* p. 4)

This internal struggle also marked Kerouac's work and eventual dissolution, the great and eternal battle destined to play out in the fields of the Lord, shaping and marking the depths of the criminal world, mapping the streets of desire and loss in the criminal city.

At Play in the Fields of the Lord by Peter Matthiessen (1965) is another important book I read in McNeil Island Federal Penitentiary and the novel captures the on the road ethos loved by criminals in the character of Moon, the part Indian man who is the protagonist.

> So long as he kept moving he would be all right. For men like himself the ends of the earth has this great allure: that one was never asked about a past or future but could live as freely as an animal, close to the gut, and day by day by day. (p. 2)

A group of us in McNeil Island undertook to read and study it and the message for us was how to be a more internally integrated criminal, how to embrace our deepest and most vital self, reflected in the title page quote opening the book:

> The way to innocence, to the uncreated and to God leads on, not back, not back to the wolf or to the child, but ever further into sin, ever deeper into human life.—Hermann Hesse.

The book is built upon *discovering* and *accepting* who you are, internally, and living your life, externally, as that, and for the central character Moon, that involved a substantial level of risk he, as did we, deemed worthy for the resulting harmony of flesh and spirit.

In the book the Catholic priest remarks to the evangelistic pastor, Martin Quarrier:

> "How is it, then, that we pass so much of our time in talk of him? Do you deny it? If he is the ordinary bandit he appears to be, why can we not dismiss him? Surely you have noticed, Senor Quarrier, that the people we dismiss most vehemently are the very ones we find it necessary to dismiss most often? And let us be honest, it is not the banditry of the late [though he was still alive they thought he wasn't] Moon that so unsettles us. We all sit up, we call old names at him; we cannot be comfortable while he is there. Yet we circle in uneasily—what is his secret, what does this man wish to know that we do not? (*Ibid.* p. 111)

We interpreted this to mean that the secret of the world was embodied in the criminal world and living as a professional criminal was what was secretly desired by all who were in the world.

The hidden history of the world, much of it revolving around private corruption of public paragons, is the history generally known within the criminal/carceral world and it is a major source—McCarthy, race, left-wing politics—which criminals, who tend to be very conservative, know the fallacy embedded in public pronouncements.

Reading about the sybarite wanderings of one of the beat elder generations in Green (1991) when the central three—Ginsberg, Burroughs and Kerouac—huddled, sprawled, wrote and intoxificated in Tangiers:

> Although Ginsberg had reported to Carr that "the only danger here is predatory leechlike guides & shoeboys & vendors of rubber spiders," Tangier still had its tense moments. Just after Allen arrived, Burroughs led his visitors straight into a riot in the Grand Socco. The local police, it seemed, had

gotten into a face-off with a band of Moroccan soldiers, and Tanjawis were taking sides. "All of a sudden a seething yelling mass of cops and soldiers and robed oldsters and blue-jeaned hoodlums came piling up the alley from wall to wall." Jack remembered. Everyone scattered, and Kerouac headed down a cul-de-sac trailing a pair of ten-year-olds who echoed his giddy laughter. Ducking into a wine shop just before the owner pulled down his shutter, he drank a glass of Malaga "as the riot boomed on by." Later, Jack found his companions sitting in an outdoor café, surveying the disorder. Burroughs, he noted, seemed peculiarly satisfied: "Riots every day," he said proudly. (p. 180)

Prison was like this, riots, or at the very least, their potential, every day, when gangs mingled in the yards, getting too close to turf, either physical, financial, or psychological, the knifes could come out, the charge across the yard or down the tier, and the explosion as they met, dealing death out with ferocious abandon, "riots every day."

Mann (1950) writes of the criminal psychology underlying the artist's work in his discussion of Nietzsche and Dostoyevsky.

"Criminal": I repeat the word, in order to indicate the psychological similarity between the cases of Nietzsche and Dostoyevsky. Not for nothing did the one feel so powerfully drawn to the other that he called him his "great teacher." The excess, the intoxicated unchaining of the understanding, in addition a religious, that is to say satanic moralism, which in Nietzsche called itself anti-moralism, that is common to them both. The epileptic's mystical sense of guilt we are told of—that was probably unknown to Nietzsche. But one of his aphorism (at the moment I cannot find it, but I definitely recall it) makes it clear that his personal feelings initiate

37

him into those of the criminal. He says in it that every intellectual segregation and estrangement from bourgeois standards, every independence and nonconformity of thought, is akin to the criminal form of existence and affords an insight into it closely approaching experience itself. I find one may go further and say that in general all creative originality, all artist nature in the broadest sense of the word, does the same. It was the French painter and sculptor Degas who said that an artist must approach his work in the spirit of the criminal about to commit his crime. (pp. 440-441)

Paralleling the theme of the Outsider described by Wilson later discussed.

Poetry, with its freedom, impressionistic, symbolic and metamorphic way of attempting to frame the truth of something so difficult to explain—the criminal and carceral reality—is the one medium virtually all criminals appreciate and whether the poetry is turned to song, read in small groups, or silently contemplated and composed, it is a potent force in prison as without and often redemptive, as this personal reflection notes:

> I have brutalized the world and she now
> Stares back at me with grim bars
> Steel and stone for the color of my heart
> And the wickedness of my ways
>
> Washed clean in the fire of Christ's blood and the dark room of the confessional
> Father intoning the timeless words
> Go in peace my son
>
> I now walk another path embraced by
> Prayer and the sonorous rhythms of the Mass
> Eyes following the finger
> Scrolling the ancient scripture
>
> David H. Lukenbill (2007)

Criminal as Philosopher

Invariably, at some point during a long stretch in prison the thought occurs in the criminal's mind, what is life about, what am I doing with my life?

Though it may be shunted aside temporarily in the daydreams of eventual release and restoration of the freedom criminal life brings when all is going well, it comes back if the right set of ideas, whether in a book or from other prison philosophers, enter into the criminal's field of vision.

The ideas have to be strong, presented with potency and clarity to even capture the attention of the criminal, and most often, initially based on a great injustice in the world that animates some of the sense of personal injustice, however unjustifiably felt, clouding the criminal's thinking.

Just such a book is *Man's Search for Meaning: An Introduction to Logotherapy,* by Viktor E. Frankl (1959).

The original title of this book was *From Death-Camp to Existentialism,* and recounted the experiences of Dr. Frankl while imprisoned in the concentration camps at Auschwitz and Dachau established by the Nazi's during the reign of Adolf Hitler.

It is a powerful book, which continues to reach out to those finding themselves in the most horrible of circumstances, with its resonating message of the fierce will to retain one's humanity, even in the most barbaric and inhuman conditions.

Studying existentialism in prison is congruent with the prison culture and it serves the purpose of beginning to study books to facilitate studying one's self.

Frankl's book is a work of existentialism, described in the Preface by Gordon W. Allport:

> It is here that we encounter the central theme of existentialism: to live is to suffer, to survive is to find meaning in the suffering. If there is a purpose in life at all, there must be a purpose in suffering and in dying. But no man can tell another what this purpose is. Each must find out for himself, and must accept the responsibility that his answer prescribes. (p. xi)

In the concentration camps, and in a maximum security prison, this message resonates with incredible depth and clarity of meaning, and if first encountered within the deepest cell in the dark prison—the great cell of solitude in the supermax facility where I first read it—it will resonate even the more deeply.

But even here, choices can still be made, to continue with brutality and the entirely predictable response to it which always punishes the brutal, either spiritually or temporally; or to choose human kindness and allow the better angels of our nature to appear in our dealings with others and perhaps find the peace so often accompanying their exhibition.

Frankl notes:

> We who lived in concentration camps can remember the men who walked through the huts comforting others, giving away their last piece of bread. They may have been few in number, but they offer sufficient proof that everything can be taken from a man but one thing: the last of the human freedoms—to choose one's attitude in any given set of circumstances, to choose one's own way. (*Ibid.* p. 65)

The Crowd by Gustave Le Bon (1952) was printed in its first English edition in 1896, but its insight about the nature and behavior of crowds in different situations, and by supposition, that of individuals, is remarkable still.

Le Bon's primary reference point was the French Revolution and the barbarity it released among the French people towards the ancient monarchy, still singular in its expression, though replicated somewhat in the Russian Revolution occurring about 20 years after this book was published.

During the period in which Le Bon is writing, the vast majority of the public was illiterate, so he was writing, as much of the writing was before the 20th Century, particularly in Europe, to his fellow well-educated members of the social elite, the ruling class.

As such there was no need to shade what he was saying and his writing is sharp and clear.

In describing what a crowd is, Le Bon notes:

> It is not necessary that a crowd should be numerous for the faculty of seeing what is taking place before its eyes to be destroyed and for the real facts to be replaced by hallucinations unrelated to them. As soon as a few individuals are gathered together they constitute a crowd, and, though, they should be distinguished men of learning, they assume all the characteristics of crowds with regard to matters outside their specialty. (p. 43)

Once gathered together, the crowd is then moved by emotion, which we see still and his description of what is used, should not be unfamiliar to those who have watched the speeches of politicians, exuberant preachers, or self-help gurus.

Le Bon remarks:

Given to exaggeration in its feelings, a crowd is only impressed by excessive sentiments. An orator wishing to move a crowd must make an abusive use of violent affirmations. To exaggerate, to affirm, to resort to repetitions, and never to attempt to prove anything by reasoning are methods of argument well known to speakers at public meetings. (*Ibid.* p. 51)

For the criminal this type of insight is rarely applied to his own actions, but to those of the herds of people populating the mass he feels he has bested, and who he feels are living lives largely constrained by rule and regulation they would willingly thwart had they the courage he has.

Consequently, much of what he reads concerning the motivation of others will be used for understanding motivation and shaping reality to more closely resemble that world he feels he has learned the truth of, the world of the criminal city, the world founded by men, not the world of the City of God.

This is not yet a place he has dared reach, nor even acknowledged exists in a potent enough way to be of concern to him and his life, but that moment is beginning to be felt.

A mention must be made here of another voice writing of crowds, mass movements; Eric Hoffer (1951) whose masterpiece, *The True Believer: Thoughts on the Nature of Mass Movements* notes.

> It sometimes seems that mass movements are custom-made to fit the needs of the criminal—not only for the catharsis of his soul but also for the exercise of his inclinations and talents. The technique of a proselytizing mass movement aims to evoke in the faithful the mood and frame of mind of a repentant criminal. Self-surrender, which

42

is...the source of a mass movement's unity and vigor, is a sacrifice, an act of atonement, and clearly no atonement is called for unless there is a poignant sense of sin....

There is a tender spot for the criminal and an ardent wooing of him in all mass movements. St. Bernard, the moving spirit of the Second Crusade, thus appealed for recruits: "For what is it but an exquisite and priceless chance of salvation due to God alone, that the omnipotent should deign to summon to His service, as though they were innocent, murderers, ravishers, adulterers, perjurers, and those guilty of every crime." ...

It is perhaps true that the criminal who embraces a holy cause is more ready to risk his life and go to extremes in its defense that people who are awed by the sanctity of life and property. (pp. 52-53)

A new book about crowds, amplifying—while differing with—much of the work of the previous two mentioned, is *The Wisdom of Crowds: Why the Many Are Smarter that the Few and How Collective Wisdom Shapes Business, Economies, Societies, and Nations*, by James Surowiecki (2004).

He writes, regarding the actions of the stock market on January 28, 1986 when the space shuttle Challenger exploded and the market, within minutes, began dumping shares of the companies who built it.

The market was smart that day because it satisfied the four conditions that characterize wise crowds: diversity of opinion (each person should have some private information, even if it's just an eccentric interpretation of the known facts), independence (people's opinions are not determined by the opinions of those around them), decentralization (people are able to specialize and draw on local knowledge), and aggregation (some mechanism exists for turning private judgments into a collective decision). If a group satisfies those conditions, its judgment is likely to be accurate. Why? At heart, the answer rests on a mathematical truism. If you ask a large enough group of diverse, independent people to make a prediction of estimate a probability, and then average those estimates, the errors each of them makes in coming up with an answer will cancel themselves out. Each person's guess, you might say, has two components: information and error. Subtract the error, and you're left with the information. (p. 10)

If the value of a life is determined by the proportion of it spent in service to others, as I believe it is, then the value of the lives of most of the avatars of the Sixties—marked by an intense self-preoccupation and virtually across the board endings more reminiscent of Gothic novels than American optimalism—has been found to not be very great, except as object lessons in how not to live a life.

Watts (1970) surely flows into this vein and his work to relativize religion—absolute truth—was very popular, and, at the time, I loved it.

He wrote:

> Those who rove freely through the various traditions, accepting what they can use and rejecting what they cannot, are condemned as undisciplined syncretists. But the use of one's reason is not a lack of discipline, nor is there any important religion which is not itself a syncretism, a "growing up together" of ideas and practices of diverse origins. (p. 61)

This creating your own thing and "doing your own thing" shaped the Sixties—though it ultimately destroyed the lives of its prophets—while validating the criminal world ethos, giving it more cultural resonance than it had ever enjoyed in the 1920's or 1930's.

Jean Paul Sartre (1963) in his seminal work, *Saint Genet*, completed the picture of mystifying the boundaries between right and wrong, creating a reality in which a child *becoming* a criminal—rather than *becoming* a being centered on divinity—is centered on a theology of criminality:

> The argument of this liturgical drama is as follows: a child dies of shame; a hoodlum rises up in his place; the hoodlum will be haunted by the child. One would have to speak of resurrection, to evoke the old initiatory rites of shamanism and secret societies, were it not that Genet refuses categorically to be a man who has been resuscitated. (p. 2)

This work is the most detailed and interesting of the works created studying the criminal. Jean Genet, criminal, poet, writer, and actor, who was also, because of Sartre's work, a well-known literary figure whose criminality was the mark of otherness that marked him for fame.

For several months in McNeil Island Federal Penitentiary, the same group of us also read and discussed this work and the broader implications of existentialism on our lives.

From that group grew a longer discussion around ideas that continued for the almost four years I was there.

Genet had embraced his being defined by the world—when caught as a child stealing—as the thief, and he became the thief, discovering in the process the delicious freedom of death of the self by embracing his defining from others, as Sartre notes:

> Having died in boyhood, Genet contains within him the dizziness of the irremediable, he wants to die

45

again. He abandons himself to the instant, to the cathartic crises that reproduce the first enchantment and carry it to the sublime: crime, capital punishment, poetry, orgasm, homosexuality. In each case we shall find the paradox of the before and after, a rise and fall, a life staked on a single card, the play of the eternal and the fleeting. (*Ibid.* p. 4)

There is, within the intensity of the point of that tipping moment during a criminal act when one's very life is at stake, when all falls on that one razor-edged moment, when one can feel that one is entering the sacred, and this moment often defines, as Sartre captured, the sublimity of the criminal life.

Genet wrote the introduction to the seminal book by George Jackson, a prisoner in San Quentin whose life and political philosophy still plays a major role in the criminal/carceral culture.

Genet writes in Jackson (1971):

If a certain complicity links the works written in prisons or asylum (Sade and Artaud share the same necessity of finding in themselves what must lead them to glory, that is, despite the walls, the moats, the jailers and the magistracy, into the light, into minds not enslaved), these works do not meet in what is still called ignominy: starting in search of themselves from the ignominy demanded by social repression, they discover common ground in the audacity of their undertaking, in the rigor and accuracy of their ideas and their visions. In prison more than elsewhere one cannot afford to be casual. One cannot endure a penalty so monstrous as the lack of freedom without demanding of one's mind and body a labour at once delicate and brutal, a labour capable of 'warping' the prisoner in a direction which takes him ever further from the social world. (pp. 18-19)

George Jackson was in Deuel Vocational Institution (DVI) from May to December of 1962, a time when I was also in DVI though I do not remember him, but the truths he was forming, are remembered.

DVI was in a particularly historic moment as the prison gangs were just beginning to take their most lethal form, and politics had seeped in.

This was an extraordinary moment in the history of the criminal/carceral world, when criminals were considered to be the vanguard of a revolution, and this moment's impact continues to strengthen criminal/carceral world culture today.

Though the search for truth from Catholicism is one of individual salvation rather than collective, its attraction to the seeker of collective liberation is powerful.

Somewhere at the root of the political truth seeker is a desire for power and there is no power greater in the world that the Catholic faith whose source is not even of this world, not even susceptible to any movements of empire or legislature, as Imperial Rome discovered.

I've always perceived liberation as a result of spiritual work rather than political, so the attractions of Karl Marx, though alluring, didn't influence me as much as those of Teilhard de Chardin.

Having entered into my intellectual studies through the door of history, I had some awareness of the failures of the collective search for freedom while the individual search proffered many stories of success.

Consequently, my reaction to the writings of Franz Fanon, Angela Davis, George Jackson, and others, was lacking in any sustained desire to become part of a collective effort, though many of the intellectual arguments had an impact on my thinking.

The idea that criminals were to be the vanguard of the revolution, so central to the writing of the California prisoners in the 1960's and 1970's, made sense to me in the context of the deep lack of any propensity for violence— clearly central to the normative Communistic theory around revolution— for most of the college-based revolutionaries I met in prison and out.

Cummins (1994) writes:

> More than any other prisoner, it had been Eldridge Cleaver who had drawn major sectors of the counterculture into the movement against California's prisons. Owing largely to this single charismatic convict, California became unique in the nation in the degree to which the prison movement came to dominate radical politics. In the Bay Area, for a large percentage of leftists, prison themes at the end of the 1960's gained prominence for a short time, even eclipsing the importance of protests late in the decade against the Vietnamese War and the broader issue of race, or even the lure of the counterculture themes of sex and drugs. And more than any other prison book, it was *Soul on Ice* that had confused these cultural radicals into thinking convicts, all convicts, were their soulmates and could be their leaders. For some extremists, the cons had become nature spirits, self-actualized, noble, violent, sexual primitives. (p. 126)

This was a sentiment shared by even the most deeply involved prison law oriented lawyers, such as Fay Stender who would many years later be murdered by an ex-convict, to write, in Pell (1972):

48

I certainly feel that, person for person, prisoners are better human beings than you would find in any random group of people. They are more loving. They have more concern or each other. They have more creative human potential. It is true that they often lose touch with reality. They are not realistic about what is potentially possible. It is very hard to convince them that they can get any sympathy or respect whatever from the system or the law. Prisoners who actually think that they can get justice from the system are usually the ones who go mad. They become unreal people, broken, deceived, deluded. (p. 13)

Collier & Horowitz (1989) writes about Stender's commitment to prison work during the Soledad Brothers—George Jackson, John Cluchette and Fleeta Drumgo—trial.

"My identity is becoming almost anti-professional," she told a student seminar in the summer of 1970, "and in some sort of way that of a political prisoner...

Such transcendental thinking involved a great leap forward, a stepping out into a territory that was intellectually undiscovered and some of her old friends thought, perhaps undiscoverable. John Irwin, a former prisoner at Soledad who had served his time and after his release obtained a degree in sociology and became a leader of the Prisoner's Union, was called into the Soledad Brothers case at about this time. Fay wanted him to listen to tape recordings made of the prisoner witnesses who would testify against Jackson and suggest ways of discrediting them. During his time at the Soledad Brothers Defense committee offices, Irwin was taken aback by the ease with which Fay and her associates accepted a sentimental and, to his way of thinking, benighted view of prisoners simply as an early warning system of the fascist state toward which all American social institutions were tending. "I don't think Fay ever understood the commitment to criminality that many of the persons she dealt with had. Fay really had a strong belief that the prisoners were going to be in the vanguard of the social revolution." Irwin was disturbed by the romantic acceptance of violent solutions and by what he saw as a kind of sexual romanticism: "It was mostly women who were doing the organizing. They had each picked their favorite Soledad Brother and were kind of oo-ing and ah-ing over them, like teenagers with movie stars. I couldn't believe it." (pp. 35-36)

This view of criminals intensified, as Cummins (1994) writes.

By the early 1970's, partially owing to Cleaver's case, [Eldridge Cleaver had taken sanctuary in Cuba in 1968 rather than go to prison] convicts who were released from California prisons frequently enjoyed instant hero status in radical organizations and often quickly assumed leadership positions. The hero worship of prisoners was most pronounced, understandably, in the cases of imprisoned Black Panther members. Betsy Carr, a movement radical who worked in the San Francisco Black Panther office in 1970 and later became the wife of ex-convict Jimmy Carr, recalls her own experience: "I got off on myths. I was completely fascinated with the Panther elite—the glamour, the bizarreness. It was my Hollywood. I'd never discussed anything with any of them, just watched in total awe." Charles Garry, Black Panther attorney, blames many of the Left's subsequent difficulties on the convict star system that this hero worship generated: "The white Left who followed the prison system...completely got mesmerized on looking upon the inmates as their heroes, and a lot of horrible mistakes were made." (pp. 146-147)

This joining of the criminal/carceral world to the world of the insiders leads inexorably to the world of *The Outsider*.

The Outsider is one of a series of books by Colin Wilson that reflects on the nexus between creativity, alienation, and society, by examining the works of various artists, like Nietzsche, Shaw, Blake, Van Gogh, Hesse, Hemingway, Camus, Nijinsky, and Gurdjieff.

Wilson proposes that it is through the work of the Outsider, those artists who have seen, who are compelled to see, reality more deeply than the common man, and by bringing their vision back to the world, help propel it upward.

The Outsiders' vision is one of a wholeness they struggle to capture in a world of broken systems and valueless cultures, and it is in the results of their search, even when failing, that the rest of us are provided glimpses of the path ahead.

Most of them fail and go mad in the failing, but the few who succeed, bring back something for us of great value, but whether it is a positive or negative value—depending on one's perspective—can be often difficult to determine.

Wilson (1956) remarks:

> The Outsider's case against society is very clear. All men and women have these dangerous, unnamable impulses, yet they keep up a pretence, to themselves, to others; their respectability, their philosophy, their religion, are all attempts to gloss over, to make look civilized and rational something that is savage, unorganized, irrational. He is an Outsider because he stands for Truth. (p.13)

The result of his study embraces the sensuality and self-ratifying seeking of the light at the center of the criminal city—occupying an ever more prominent place in its burning towers, even to the penthouse—and for criminals fabricating their perspective for deeper penetration into the criminal world, it is a dark light indeed.

Wilson concludes:

> There are still many difficulties that cannot be touched on here. The problem for the 'civilization' is the adoption of a religious attitude that can be assimilated as *objectively* as the headlines of last Sunday's newspapers. But the problem for the individual always will be the opposite of this, the conscious striving *not* to limit the amount of experience seen and touched; the intolerable struggle to expose the sensitive areas of being to what may possibly hurt them; the attempt to see as a whole, although the instinct of self-preservation fights against the pain of the internal widening, and all the impulses of spiritual laziness build into waves of sleep with each new effort. The individual begins that long effort as an Outsider; he may finish it as a saint. (p. 281)

Wilson's book and the foundational ideas seemingly so congruent with those of many other writers and thinkers who loved the notion of being considered an Outsider, vaulted him into the rarefied atmosphere of the other avatars of the Sixties, from which the same reviewers of his work that placed him there, tried to remove him, but he is still, as of this writing—November 2012—alive and writing, as this article by Hillman (2011) notes.

> Colin Wilson – one of the Angry Young Men of the 1950s – turned eighty with the approbation of his devotees ringing in his ears, but hardly a whisper from those who set themselves up as arbiters of English writing....

The reasons for Fleet Street's coolness towards one of Britain's most remarkable writers of modern times are complex, but no less shameful for that.

A novelist, essayist, polemicist, philosopher and science fiction writer has who toiled at his keyboard every day of the year – and that includes Christmas Day – since the mid-1950s, gathering an international following that is almost slavish in its adulation, deserves his due as he soldiers on into his ninth decade.

But the occasion passed virtually unremarked except by those – the readers of his incredible range of work – who see Wilson as a literary phenomenon unparalleled in the entire history of English letters. A celebratory book of essays was published to mark the day, but there was nothing like the kind of coverage his huge output warranted.

Wilson rose to fame alongside the playwright John Osborne in 1956 when his book, The Outsider, was published by Victor Gollancz just as Osborne's groundbreaking play, Look Back in Anger, opened at the Royal Court Theatre in London.

Together, they became part of a mythical literary brotherhood known by the popular press as The Angry Young Men. John Braine, Kingsley Amis, John Wain and Alan Sillitoe became fellow members of the group, which went on to dominate the course of English fiction for several years thereafter.

Wilson's book, which drew heavily on the work of prominent philosophers to identify the role of the outsider in modern society, was initially lauded to the skies by prominent Sunday paper critics of the time. They noted, in particular, his precocity (he was only 24) and his unlikely background as a working class lad from Leicester who had never been to university. (np)

The mystical way so many thought was a deep penetration of the profoundest level of truth, emerged then from the drug culture—as it had so many times before in so many different guises—resonating with the Sixties seeker and taking its deepest root in the theory of the game.

One of the most seductive presentations of the game theory map of life was *The Master Game,* by Robert De Ropp which defined the scripts and traps of the many ways the seeker could lose, and then ultimately find, his truest and highest self.

Tied in to the existential praxis and Esalenistic therapeutic theories, it took the position that what we really needed to make our lives complete and fulfilling was a game worth playing and several were presented, high and low.

De Ropp (1968) defined nine games and their aims:

Table 1
Meta-games and Object Games

Game	Aim
Master Game	awakening
Religion Game	salvation
Science Game	knowledge
Art Game	beauty
Householder Game	raise family
No Game	no aim
Hog in Trough	wealth
Cock on Dunghill	fame
Moloch Game	glory or victory (p. 13)

Game theory is so congruent with the criminal world that many times the street/prison query, "What is your game?" is asked; contrasting to "What do you do?" heard in the suburban lounges where the non-criminal world congregates, though both are driven by the still unconscious values of acquisition and success at any cost, foundational to the criminal city.

Many of the paradigms of thought endemic to various forms of human interaction are based on the dog-eat-dog reality of the perceived world, often labeled *real* politics, get *real,* and so on.

And this is what game theory is based on, the *real* versus the illusion, and should you subscribe to it, you then become *real,* an illusion no longer.

Part of becoming *real* is discovering the truth about humanity that lie behind the illusion, and for that one needs the key.

De Ropp notes:

> In the previous chapter man was compared to the inhabitant of a house containing locked rooms, "vast chambers full of treasures with windows looking out on eternity and infinity." It was said that man in general does not enter these locked rooms. He has lost the key. Sometimes he suspects that the rooms are there and may try to unlock the doors by the use of drugs. More often he does not even know that the rooms exist. (*Ibid.* p. 49)

The greatest expression of the spiritual potency of life as game is *Magister Ludi*—which I'll mention later—by Herman Hesse, the author who captivated so many of us during the Sixties, and rereading his autobiographical novel, *Steppenwolf*—which I first read in prison while still in my twenties, passing over the injunction that it was written by Hesse at fifty and meant for readers in their fifties—know that I became that man in some fashion as I absorbed the animating cores of so many of the books I read deeply, as all books are read in prison, deeply.

For all of us, the dark and dour men who struggle with their own interpretations of how life has caused them to suffer and how it is so unworthy of our ideals, yet, with our own Maria/Hermine safely at our side, showing us through her lived life, the indescribable joys of the daily comings and goings, the sun and flowers and bees dancing through red roses.

Hesse (1963) writes of the attraction between male and female criminals, outsiders, outlaws:

> "I know," she said..."I shall make you fall in love with me, but there's no use hurrying. First of all we're comrades, two people who hope to be friends, because we have recognized each other. For the present we'll each learn from the other and amuse ourselves together. I show you my little stage, and teach you to dance and to have a little pleasure and be silly; and you show me your thoughts and something of all you know."

> "There's little there to show you, Hermine, I'm afraid. You know far more that I do. You're a most remarkable person—and a woman. But do I mean anything to you? Don't I bore you?"

> She looked down darkly to the floor.

> "That's how I don't like to hear you talk. Think of that evening when you came broken from your despair and loneliness, to cross my path and be my comrade. Why was it, do you think, I was able to recognize you and understand you?"

> "Why, Hermine? Tell me!"

> "Because it's exactly the same for me as for you, because I am alone exactly as you are, because I'm as little fond of life and men and myself as you are

and can put up with them as little. There are always a few such people who demand the utmost of life and yet cannot come to terms with its stupidity and crudeness." (p. 141)

During that wonderful first night and the days that followed Maria taught me much. She taught me the charming play and delights of the senses, but she gave me, also, new understanding, new insight, new love. (*Ibid*. p. 156)

Pope Benedict XVI, likes Hesse's writing and considers *Steppenwolf* one of his favorites, as this book consisting of the cardinal being interviewed, written when he was still Joseph Cardinal Ratzinger (1997) notes.

> [Interviewer] Steppenwolf *is among your favorite books. The novel is considered one of the most significant documents of cultural pessimism and early existentialism. On rereading it, one finds the record of a neurotically hypersensitive person, whose agonizing self-analysis is at the same time the attempt to diagnose the illness of the time. Does this description also have something to do with you?*
>
> [Ratzinger] No. For me the book was a real discovery because of its diagnostic and prognostic power. It anticipated, in a certain way, the problems that we subsequently lived through in the sixties and seventies. The novel, as you know, is actually about one person, but one who analyzes himself into so many personalities that the analysis finally leads to self-disintegration. Stretching the self too far here also means destroying it. In other words, there aren't just two souls in one breast; man disintegrates altogether. I didn't' read this to identify with it but as a key that with visionary power pierces through and exposes the problem of

modernity's isolated and self-isolating man. (Italics in original, p. 70)

Magister Ludi attracted me because its common name, *The Bead Game* was congruent with my thinking at the time—mid 1960's in McNeil Island Federal Penitentiary—I read it, that life was a game.

In describing the bead game's rules, Hesse (1967) wrote:

> One only learns the playing rules of this game of games in the usual prescribed ways—the result of many years' experience—and none of the initiated could have the least possible interest in making its rules easier of acquisition.

> These rules, the symbols and grammar of the Game, represent a type of highly developed, secret language, in which several sciences and arts, in particular mathematics and music (not to forget the theory of music), play their part, and which are capable of expressing the contents and results of nearly all the sciences and of placing them in relation to each other. The Bead Game is also a device that comprises the complete contents and values of our culture; it plays with them, as in the springtime of the arts, a painter may have toyed with the colours of his palette. All that mankind, in creative periods, has produced in the field of beliefs, elevated thoughts and works of art, all that the ensuing periods have furnished in scholarly observation and concept and consolidated into intellectual property, will be utilized by the Bead Game adept. (pp. 16-17)

In rereading the book today, I realize that the bead game has been and is played, though for real, by our greatest Catholic philosophers and theologians—in harmony with the Church by St. Thomas Aquinas and disharmoniously by Teilhard de Chardin and Leonardo Boff—because they have access, through the history and teaching of the Church; "All that mankind, in creative periods, has produced in the field of beliefs, elevated thoughts and works of art, all that the ensuing periods have furnished in scholarly observation and concept and consolidated into intellectual property," and of these the greatest is surely St. Thomas Aquinas, so I was somewhat floored when the first historical personage mentioned by name and context, by Hesse in the book is the Angelic Doctor.

> One thing is certain: what we today understand by "personality" is very different from that which biographers and historians of earlier times understood by it. For them, namely for the authors of those periods—authors who possessed an unveiled penchant for biography—it appears, one might almost say, that the important ingredients of a personality were deviation, abnormality and originality—often to the point of pathology—whereas we of today only speak of personalities when we meet with men who are beyond all originalities and peculiarities and who have succeeded in achieving the most perfect possible self-identification with the general, and in rendering the most perfect possible service to the supra-personal.

> When we examine this more closely, we see that the concept was already known to Antiquity—the figure of the "Sage" or "Perfect One" for example in Ancient China, and the ideal of the Socratic doctrine of virtue, can hardly be distinguished from our modern ideal. Many great spiritual organisations, too, such as the Roman Church in its mightiest epochs, knew similar fundamental truths, and many of its greatest figures, *vide* St. Thomas Aquinas, appear to us like early Greek sculptures, classical representatives of types rather than individuals. (*Ibid.* pp. 14-15)

Pope Benedict XVI, while still Joseph Cardinal Ratzinger, (1997) commented on *The Bead Game,* in an interview made into a book.

> [Interviewer] *Is it possible to play at theology like a game, in the way that Hermann Hesse described in his* The Glass Bead Game?
>
> [Ratzinger] That would be too little. I mean, there is certainly an element of playfulness. But ultimately, it's not, as Hesse thinks in *The Glass Bead Game*, a question of a constructed world, a sort of mathematics of thinking, but of confronting reality. And by that I mean the whole compass and the whole claim of reality. To that extent, the element of play is included, because it is, after all, an authentic element of our existence, a component, but it wouldn't be enough to characterize the right way of doing theology. (p. 69)

The Bead Game fascinated me for its reduction of all and everything to one system, which I finally discovered existed only, completely and fully, in the Sacred Doctrine of the Catholic Church.

Another synthesizer was Antoine De Saint-Exupery, the great French author and pilot who died while on a military flight during World War II, gained fame as the author of *The Little Prince*, a fable about a little boy containing profound truths for adults, but his real claim to fame among the wisdom seekers in the criminal world is his magnum opus *The Wisdom of the Sands,* which is a powerful and magnificent statement about the essential nobility and grandeur of man.

Saint-Exupery (1950) opens *Wisdom of the Sands*:

> All too often have I seen pity led astray. But we who govern men have learnt to plumb their hearts, and we bestow compassion only on what is worthy of

our concern. No pity waste I on the shrilly voiced afflictions that fret women's hearts. As I withhold it from the dying and from the dead. And I know wherefore.

A time there was, in my young days, when I pitied beggars and their sores. I hired physicians and procured balsams for them. Caravans from a far-off island brought me those rare unguents laced with gold that mend the torn skin above the flesh. Thus did I until the day when I discovered that beggars cling to their stench as to something rare and precious. For I had caught them scratching away their scabs and smearing their bodies with dung, like the husbandman who spreads manure over his garden plot, so as to wean from it the crimson flower. (p. 3)

This clarity and insight resonates today, and its deep footsteps tracking across the endless desert sands of our modern world where the forlorn are mourned beyond recompense and their cries reach eternity, as endless as the sands their lives sleep upon, reminding us of what is solid, built on rock, built upon Peter.

Saint-Exupery was a devout Catholic who refined his spiritual perspective from his experiences in the Saharan Desert, revealing to us another and deeper vision of the great City of God—paradoxically and imaginatively built upon the shifting desert sands— which stands forever against the willow world of the city of men.

He notes:

> For I have lit upon a great truth: to wit, that all men *dwell*, and life's meaning changes for them with the meaning of the home. And that roads, barley-fields and hillsides look different to a man according as they belong, or do not belong, to a domain. For once we feel that these divers things are bound

together in a whole, then and only then, do they make an imprint on our hearts. Likewise, he who dwells and he who dwells not in the Kingdom of God do not inhabit the same universe. They are befooled in their own conceit, the unbelievers, who mock at us as dreamers, fondly thinking that the riches they seek are tangible. When they covet another's flocks or herds, it is but to gratify their pride; and the joys of pride are of the spirit and intangible. (*Ibid.* p. 15)

Life's meaning is shaped by the interior mansions richly adorned, the empty deserts resolutely traversed, and the beckoning sunlit skies our open hands grasp; embraced deeply and eternally.

Exupery's work, of such fierce beauty, resonates with the criminal bound within the prison of stone and steel, for it carves velvet soft and wondrous love from such bleakness.

Saint-Exupery bridges philosophy and religion with his soaring speculations on the paradoxes of life which he contemplated most often during his flights, particularly across the deserts of Africa, where he disappeared—and it is presumed he died—on July 31, 1944 while flying reconnaissance for the Allies to determine if there were any German troop movements in the region.

The fervent philosophy of the desert prince, who was his protagonist in *The Wisdom of the Sands,* resonates deeply with men involved in life or death situations on a daily basis, whether it is from combat duty in the military or the normal razor-edge of life within the criminal/carceral world.

It is a stark philosophy, hard, clear, and resolute; where each act is reflected in the glare of impending death from any mistaken movement, or uncertainty when certainty is the only option.

It is a philosophy of absolutes. Things are. You act accordingly. Hesitation is weakness and ultimate disaster, which may come immediately or years later.

Saint-Exupery's gift was to have tried to live this way—a new biography, *Saint –Exupery: A Biography,* by Stacy Schiff (1994) is excellent—to have contemplated his life deeply, and to have written about it, inspiring others with his thoughts.

In a world of relativity, the attraction of this type of clarity is enormous to those who live the harrowing lives its profundity is built upon.

Another writer whose works, perhaps most led me directly to Catholicism, were those by Taylor Caldwell, and most of all, her greatest work, in my opinion; *A Pillar of Iron*, about Cicero of Rome, but who many assumed it was also about the United States.

She writes of a meeting between Marcus Cicero, Julius Caesar, Crassus and Pompey:

> Julius clasped his thin dark hands on the table and looked steadfastly at Marcus.
>
> "You know some of the power of Catilina, whom we despise but whom we dare not ignore. We have spoken of freedmen, slaves and petty criminals who are his followers. In themselves, they are not too dangerous. But they are not the sole supporters of our patrician friend. There are ambitious men who are his familiars, Piso and Curius to name only two. He also has many Senators and tribunes in his pay, or their secret crimes are known to him. Besides these, there are the tens of thousands of athletes in Rome, and men of unutterable but powerful evil who make their living on vice. There are the malcontents, and do not underestimate them, for they are legion! There are men, multitudes of them,

who are not Romans, but who are rich. Their loyalty is not to Rome, but to their own service. There are men who make treason their profession, for they hate Rome and the symbol which is Rome, and desire despotism.

"Among these of the disaffected is the great patrician class, who despise the Republic, and who wish to rule an enslaved nation. These have multitudes of clients who would obey their masters, who would obey their masters, who would obey Catilina, who is one o f them.

"There are the gutter rabble, obsessed with greed and the gratification of their bellies and their lusts. What is Rome to them, and Rome's solvency? They would betray her for a free pot of beans, or two tickets to the circus. Then there are the motley creatures of hideous, depraved appetites, and actors and songsters and dancers, who love to shriek in the wake of patrician and royal authority for the light that falls on them. There are the homosexuals and other perverts who writhe with joy at the thought of exploitation and whips, and the promise of legal protection.

"These are the followers of Catilina, Marcus. These are the ones who at his word would destroy our nation." ...

Marcus stood up slowly. He looked from one to the other. "My reason tells me that you speak the truth. Nevertheless, my spirit insists that I fight that truth, that I do what I can to make men more than he is. Long before our time the customs of our ancestors molded admirable men, and in turn these eminent men upheld the ways and institutions of their forebears. Our age, however, inherited the Republic like some beautiful painting of bygone days, its colors already fading through great age;

and not only has our time neglected to freshen the colors of the picture, but we have failed to preserve it form and outlines. For what remains to us nowadays, of the ancient ways on which the commonwealth, we were told, was founded? We see them so lost in oblivion that they are not merely neglected but quite forgot. And what am I to say of you? Our customs have perished for want of men to stand by them, and we are called to an account, so that we stand impeached like men accused of capital crimes, compelled to plead our own cause. Through our vices, rather than from fate, we retain the word 'Republic' long after we have lost the reality."

He spread out his hands mutely, then added, "I, too, am guilty. I stand before you guilty men, a guilty man, myself. I have no defense except that, at least, I have tried, if to no avail." (pp. 428-430)

In reading about Taylor Caldwell on Wikipedia, it is clear her final days were not so good, and her infatuation with strident conservatism—she wrote articles for the John Birch Society (whose blandishments I also succumbed to temporarily after being invited to join by a cousin who was an officer of the organization)—and reincarnation did not mesh to her benefit.

The dynamic duo of Laing & Szasz turned it all upside down with their consensus that mental illness was a sane response to an insane culture; which to criminals became: "becoming a criminal in a criminal culture is a smart move."

I read the book by R.D. Laing (1967), *The Politics of Experience*, after I had been released from prison and it corroborated the ideas—from a psychotherapeutic position—which I had been reading and thinking about for years, and really blew the lid off with its contention (putting a bow around the other ideas promoting disorder and chaos loose in the culture) that the people labeled insane were really sane:

> In over 100 cases where we studied the actual circumstances around the social event when one person comes to be regarded as schizophrenic, it seems to us that *without exception* the experience and behavior that gets labeled schizophrenia is *a special strategy that a person invents in order to live in an unlivable situation.* (pp. 78-79, italics in original)

> There is no such "condition" as "schizophrenia," but the label is a social fact and the social fact a *political event.* This political event, occurring in the civic order of society, imposes definitions and consequences on the labeled person. It is a social prescription that rationalizes a set of social actions whereby the labeled person is annexed by others, who are legally sanctioned, medically empowered and morally obliged, to become responsible for the person labeled. The person labeled is inaugurated not only into a role, but into a career of patient, by the concerted action of a coalition (a "conspiracy") of family, G. P., mental health officer, psychiatrists, nurses, psychiatric social workers, and often fellow patients. The "committed" person labeled as a patient, and specifically as "schizophrenic," is degraded from full existential and legal status as human agent and responsible person to someone no longer in possession of his own definition of himself, unable to retain his own possessions, precluded from the exercise of his discretion as to whom he meets, what he does. His time is no longer his own and the space he occupies is no longer of his choosing. After being subjected to a degradation ceremonial known as psychiatric examination, he is bereft of his civil liberties in being imprisoned in a total institution known as a "mental" hospital. More completely, more radically than anywhere else in

our society, he is invalidated as a human being. In the mental hospital he must remain, until the label is rescinded or qualified by such terms as "remitted" or "readjusted." Once a "schizophrenic," there is a tendency to be regarded as always a "schizophrenic." (*Ibid.* pp. 83-84)

It takes absolutely no imagination at all to see how this can be folded into a justification and experience of the criminal through his experience in the criminal/carceral world.

I carried and spread this ideology around for years and it wasn't until I entered into the deepest discussion with the Catholic Church as the sign of contradiction, that the argument finally became obsolete.

The last book I read before being released from McNeil Island Federal Penitentiary in 1969 was *The Temptation to Exist* by E. M. Cioran (1968) whose very opening spoke to criminals.

> Almost all our discoveries are due to our violences, to the exacerbation of our instability. Even God, insofar as He interests us—it is not in our innermost selves that we discern God, but at the extreme limits of our fever, at the very point where, our rage confronting His, a shock results, an encounter as ruinous for Him as for us. Blasted by the curse attached to acts, the man of violence forces his nature, rises above himself only to relapse, an aggressor, followed by his enterprises, which come to punish him for having instigated them. Every work turns against its author: the poem will crush the poet, the system the philosopher, the event the man of action. Destruction awaits anyone who, answering to his vocation and fulfilling it, exerts himself within history; only the man who sacrifices every gift and talent escapes: released from his humanity, he may lodge himself in Being. (p. 33)

Of all the writers who expressed a philosophic position, whether within a fiction or nonfiction vehicle, the one who had one of the most powerful impacts on me was the fellow Russian Jew, Alissa Zinovievna Rosenbaum, born in St. Petersburg February 2, 1905, who later, in one of the most triumphal accounts of personal transformation in the 20th Century, became Ayn Rand.

My grandmother, Lillian Oren, was a Ukrainian Jew, who, in adapting to America, was a non-practicing Jew, and married my grandfather, Wesley Hewitt, an English, Scot, salesman and real estate investor; but it was not until many years later, during our exploration of Judaism prior to becoming Catholic, that I discovered my Jewish heritage.

My first reading of Ayn Rand was *The Fountainhead*, in a dark, dingy, dirty, cell in Ogden City Jail while being transferred from Salt Lake City Jail—where I was imprisoned for escaping from the Nevada State Reformatory in Elko, Nevada—to the Federal Correctional Institution in Englewood, Colorado.

I read the fat, scruffy paperback in one great gulp, and embraced it, as the complete self-centered, individualistic philosophy that is—at its axial core—deeply criminal, and my thief's heart reveled at the harmonious congruence, though I could only relate in dreams with Rand's protagonist's lives of high drama and high finance.

It was in her thought, especially as expressed in *The Virtue of Selfishness: A New Concept of Egoism* (1964), that I first found elevated ideas central to the American experience which corresponded to my very limited knowledge and experience of that America; which from my prison cell looked like the interior world she described.

> The capacity to experience pleasure or pain is innate in a man's body; it is part of his *nature*, part

of the kind of entity he *is*. He has no choice about it, and he has no choice about the standard that determines what will make him experience the physical sensation of pleasure or of pain. What is that standard? *His life*.

The pleasure-pain mechanism in the body of man—and in the bodies of all the living organisms that possess the faculty of consciousness—serves as an automatic guardian of the organism's life. The physical sensation of pleasure is a signal indicating that the organism is pursuing the *right* course of action. The physical sensation of pain is a warning signal of danger, indicating that the organism is pursuing the *wrong* course of action, that something is impairing the proper function of its body, which requires action to correct it. (p. 8, Italics in original)

She was, and remains, a major American philosopher, who was clearly an atheist, but as I just learned recently, felt a certain collegial kinship with the greatest Catholic theologian, as Sciabarra (1995) discovered.

In this book I also make explicit comparisons and distinctions between Rand and other social thinkers. This is often a difficult task, owing partly to Rand's myopia concerning both her intellectual debts and her assessment of other philosophers. In bravura fashion, Rand once said that in the history of philosophy, she could only recommend the "3A's"—Aristotle, Aquinas and Ayn Rand. (p. 12)

Rand's work shares the sense of clear absolutes that I have always found so attractive in Exupery's *Wisdom of the Sands*, but while his is universal and deeply mystical, hers is only in America and deeply practical, while built upon ideas that are as sweepingly mystical as his.

I have come to believe that if Rand could have come into contact with comparable Catholic thinkers early in her life, she would have become one of the great Catholic philosophers because so many of her ideas radiate traditional Catholicism and that is why so many current Catholics are reading her.

When I read now two of the thinkers who have had a great influence on my thinking, Rand and Abraham Maslow, it is clear that all good thinkers who discover truth and see it reflected through their eyes and through the lens of their knowledge and experience, have discovered some aspect of Catholic truth and we know this because the Lord came to earth and told us: "I am the way, and the truth, and the life." (John 14:6)

Read how eloquently Rand (1964) describes racism in a truly unique way I have never read anywhere else.

> Racism is the lowest, most crudely primitive form of collectivism. It is the notion of ascribing moral, social or political significance to a man's genetic lineage—the notion that a man's intellectual and characterological traits are produced and transmitted by his internal body chemistry. Which means, in practice, that a man is to be judged, not by his won character and actions, but by the characters and actions of a collective of ancestors.

> Racism claims that the content of a man's mind (not his cognitive apparatus, but its *content*) is inherited; that a man's convictions, values and character are determined before he is born, by physical factors beyond his control. This is the caveman's version of the doctrine of innate ideas— or of inherited knowledge—which has been thoroughly refuted by philosophy and science. Racism is a doctrine of, by and for brutes. It is a barn-yard or stock-farm version of collectivism, appropriate to a mentality that differentiates

between various breeds of animals, but not between animals and men. (p. 172, Italics in original)

It is here and in so many other ways that she makes a clear distinction between man and animals that she reveals her unspoken underlying acknowledgment of the absolute eternal, which in any form shaped, points towards God; which if, again, exposed to the subtle thought of a John Courtenay Murray, or even more appropriate, Father John McCloskey, the influential Opus Dei priest, might have made a Catholic out of her.

However, anyone reading Rand's blistering denunciation of the 1967 Encyclical from Pope Paul VI, *Populorum Progressio* (On the Development of Peoples) would conclude that becoming Catholic would be impossible for her, regardless of the brilliance of the evangelists.

Rand (1967) wrote:

> The encyclical is the manifesto of an impassioned hatred for capitalism; but its evil is much more profound and its target is more than mere politics. It is written in terms of a mystic-altruist "sense of life." A sense of life is the subconscious equivalent of metaphysics: a pre-conceptual, emotionally integrated appraisal of man's nature and of his relationship to existence. To a mystic-altruist sense of life, words are mere approximations; hence the encyclical's tone of evasion. But what is eloquently revealing is the nature of that which is being evaded. (p. 340)

Populorum Progressio is one part of the Lampstand Foundation's social magisterium informing our work, which we embraced following its inclusion in Pope Benedict's XVI (2005) Encyclical *Deus Caritas Est*

> 27. It must be admitted that the Church's leadership was slow to realize that the issue of the

just structuring of society needed to be approached in a new way. There were some pioneers, such as Bishop Ketteler of Mainz († 1877), and concrete needs were met by a growing number of groups, associations, leagues, federations and, in particular, by the new religious orders founded in the nineteenth century to combat poverty, disease and the need for better education. In 1891, the papal magisterium intervened with the Encyclical *Rerum Novarum* of Leo XIII. This was followed in 1931 by Pius XI's Encyclical *Quadragesimo Anno*. In 1961 Blessed John XXIII published the Encyclical *Mater et Magistra*, while Paul VI, in the Encyclical *Populorum Progressio* (1967) and in the Apostolic Letter *Octogesima Adveniens* (1971), insistently addressed the social problem, which had meanwhile become especially acute in Latin America. My great predecessor John Paul II left us a trilogy of social Encyclicals: *Laborem Exercens* (1981), *Sollicitudo Rei Socialis* (1987) and finally *Centesimus Annus* (1991). Faced with new situations and issues, Catholic social teaching thus gradually developed, and has now found a comprehensive presentation in the *Compendium of the Social Doctrine of the Church* published in 2004 by the Pontifical Council *Iustitia et Pax*. Marxism had seen world revolution and its preliminaries as the panacea for the social problem: revolution and the subsequent collectivization of the means of production, so it was claimed, would immediately change things for the better. This illusion has vanished. In today's complex situation, not least because of the growth of a globalized economy, the Church's social doctrine has become a set of fundamental guidelines offering approaches that are valid even beyond the confines of the Church: in the face of ongoing development these guidelines need to be addressed in the context of dialogue with all those seriously concerned for humanity and for the world in which we live. (#27)

Pope Paul VI's (1967) encyclical is most certainly not anti-capitalist, nor evil in any form, but written in the universal form of papal encyclicals written for—in addition for all Catholics—for all men and women of good will in the world, and a few excerpts regarding the key element of capitalism, personal responsibility and it's greatest enemy, collectivism and centrally-planned economies, make the point.

> 15. In God's plan, every man is born to seek self-fulfillment, for every human life is called to some task by God. At birth a human being possesses certain aptitudes and abilities in germinal form, and these qualities are to be cultivated so that they may bear fruit. By developing these traits through formal education or personal effort, the individual works his way toward the goal set for him by the Creator.

> Endowed with intellect and free will, each man is responsible for his self-fulfillment even as he is for his salvation. He is helped, and sometimes hindered, by his teachers and those around him; yet whatever be the outside influences exerted on him, he is the chief architect of his own success or failure. Utilizing only his talent and willpower, each man can grow in humanity, enhance his personal worth, and perfect himself. (#15)

> 33. Individual initiative alone and the interplay of competition will not ensure satisfactory development. We cannot proceed to increase the wealth and power of the rich while we entrench the needy in their poverty and add to the woes of the oppressed. Organized programs are necessary for "directing, stimulating, coordinating, supplying and integrating" the work of individuals and intermediary organizations.

It is for the public authorities to establish and lay down the desired goals, the plans to be followed, and the methods to be used in fulfilling them; and it is also their task to stimulate the efforts of those involved in this common activity. But they must also see to it that private initiative and intermediary organizations are involved in this work. In this way they will avoid total collectivization and the dangers of a planned economy which might threaten human liberty and obstruct the exercise of man's basic human rights. (#33)

Rand's aversion to Catholicism might stem, in my opinion, to the experience she had growing up in Russia and seeing the much-too-close relationship between the Communists and Russian Orthodoxy, noted by Sciabarra (1995).

Alexey Khomyakov [19th Century Russian intellectual] embraced the Slavophile devotion to Orthodox Christianity and personal mystical experience. He viewed Russian orthodoxy, with its Byzantine roots, as the reconciliation of Catholicism and Protestantism. N. O. Lossky, Rand's teacher and author of the indispensible *History of Russian Philosophy*, explains that for Khomyakov, "the rationalism of Catholicism which established unit without freedom gave rise, as a reaction against it, to another form of rationalism—Protestantism which realizes freedom without unity". Khomyakov saw the necessity for a communal, conciliar unity that transcended the Catholic emphasis on the individual judgement of the believer. Russian Orthodoxy bound the Church and the state much more closely than was the case in the West. (pp. 26-27)

How frightening close was not fully and publicly revealed until much later, as Weigel (2010) notes:

> On September 5, 1978, the new pope [John Paul I]
> received [Russian Orthodox] Metropolitan Nikodim
> of Leningrad, one of the six presidents of the World
> Council of Churches and a man who struck many
> Westerners as deeply pious. The KGB knew
> Nikodim as ADAMANT, as it knew his secretary,
> Nikolai Lvovich Tserpitsky (code name
> VLADIMIR). At the end of his private audience
> with John Paul, ADAMANT suffered a massive
> heart attack and died in the Pope's arms. John Paul
> I later remarked that Nikodim had spoken "the
> most beautiful words about the Church I have ever
> heard" during their meeting; his last words, as the
> Pope held the fallen bishop, were said to have been
> "I am not a KGB agent." But he was. (p. 99)

But, surely people living in Russia would have known that
the Orthodox was under the control of the government,
and if anything would have added fuel to the anti-religious
fire burning within the breast of young Ayn Rand, this
surely would have.

And yet, reading her book, Anthem (2010), we find an
expression of the eternal truth of the individual that is at
its core, Catholic.

> I stand here on the summit of the mountain. I lift
> my head and I spread my arms. This, my body and
> spirit, this is the end of the quest. I wished to know
> the meaning of things. I am the meaning. I wished
> to find a warrant for being. I need no warrant for
> being, and no word of sanction upon my being. I
> am the warrant and the sanction. (p. 94)

I first encountered Abraham Maslow in a psychology class
at Sacramento City College in 1973, and once studying his
theory of self-actualization, realized that here was an
intellect that saw the beauty of life and love of work rather
than horror or drudgery as the over-arcing narrative.

I bought his book on management, *Eupsychian Management: A Journal*, (1965) in 1974 when I was receiving funding for a federal grant to reform criminals through exposure to college education and peer-counseling and would be managing 13 people, something I had never done before.

From the very first paragraphs, I saw personal reference points in my upcoming work.

> We can learn from self-actualizing people what the ideal attitude toward work might be under the most favorable circumstances. These highly evolved individuals assimilate their work into the identity, into the self, i.e., work actually becomes part of the self, part of the individual's definition of himself. Work can be psychotherapeutic, psychogogic (making well people grow toward self-actualization). This of course is a circular relationship to some extent, i.e., given fairly o.k. people to begin with, in a fairly good organization, then work tends to improve the people. This tends to improve the industry, which in turn tends to improve the people involved, and so it goes. [And this final line is the first line I marked in my copy still in my library.] This is the simplest way of saying that proper management of the work lives of human beings, of the way in which they earn their living, can improve them and improve the world and in this sense be a utopian or revolutionary technique. (p. 1)

Maslow (1999) use of the term eupsychian is described:

> Maslow coined the term "eupsychian" (from the Greek prefix *eu-*, meaning good, well, true) as an extension of "utopian." The point of the extension was that human life and society could be perfected only in the degree that we understand and take

account of the realities of basic human needs. (p. 124. *n.*)

Central to the idea of the self-actualizing human being is the peak experience, which he writes about (1971).

> We have made studies of peak experiences by asking groups of people and individuals such questions as, What was the most ecstatic moment of your life? ...Have you experienced transcendent ecstasy?...

> In our investigations of peak experiences, we found many, many triggers, many kinds of experiences that would set them off. Apparently most people, or almost all people, have peak experiences, or ecstasies....I want to report that the two easiest ways of getting peak experiences (in terms of simple statistics in empirical reports) are through music and through sex.....

> So far, I have found that these peak experiences are reported from what we might call "classical music." I have not found a peak experience from John Cage or from an Andy Warhol movie, from abstract-expressionistic kind of painting, or the like. I just haven't. (pp. 174-176)

This justified my drug taking and sexual proclivities for many years until I realized that the *truth* of peak experiences was inner congruence with the truth of my life, which was built upon God and his Church, all else was a mirage of the world and its prince.

Criminal As Religious

The Transcendentalist, an essay given by Ralph Waldo Emerson in the Masonic Temple in 1842 resonates deeply with Americans, particularly those in the criminal world familiar with its eloquent expression of reliance on self as the final arbiter of individual destiny and creation.

Emerson (1983) notes:

> Do not cumber yourself with fruitless pains to men and remedy remote effects; let the soul be erect, and all things will go well. You think me the child of my circumstances: I make my circumstance." (p. 196)

This stance is deeply religious in its definition of the individual soul as divine, and in no need of divinity beyond it, but whose only pursuit should be to understand and grasp its essential nature.

Concerning nature and spirit Emerson remarks:

> Nature is not fixed but fluid. Spirit alters, moulds, makes it. The immobility or bruteness of nature, is the absence of spirit; to pure spirit, it is fluid, it is volatile, it is obedient. Every spirit builds itself a house; and beyond its house a world; and beyond its world, a heaven. Know then that the world exists for you." (*Ibid.* p. 48)

The essence of the criminal city is self, all revolves around the satisfying of the desires of self, however attained, and what has once been virtue may now be crime, and so the opposite.

The completely self-focused spirituality often appeals to those enamored of the more global holistically focused spiritualities, as did Emerson with his Unitarian background and his strong attraction to Buddhism.

They see nature as alive in a conscious way, reducing humanity and themselves to a simple part of creation, rather than the crown of creation, reducing God to a nymph in the woods or a satyr on a tree stump playing pipes, and all the old pagan personages roll back into view, swamping us once again in their shallow relativity and endless bickering.

Born in the protestations of the Reformation and the break with the Catholic Church, the Babel of faiths and creeds that sprung forth, building on already primal roots, and Emerson, ever the seeker of his own myth, constructed an entire career and scholarly life upon their wobbly foundations, wherein many criminals find spiritual succor and weighty rationalizations for creating a way of life that perceives no absolutes, only self and the endless games self plays.

The New Golden Bough, which orders and blends new research material into the 1890 classic of Sir James Frazer, explores the ground upon which, to the still learning eye, the reality of later religious and organizational truths have been constructed; and its opening tale of the King of the Wood—a tale I shared many times with my fellow prisoners—whose sovereignty was passed through the execution of the reigning king by a usurper, approximates that of how the leadership of criminal and carceral world gangs often passes to a new generation.

And in its deeper explorations of the passages of gods, whose births, deaths and resurrections, congruent with the passage of the seasons from fertile to barren and back again; the myths of the prince of this world attempt to destroy the truths of its Lord. Frazer (1959) notes:

*"If the high gods, who dwell remote from the fret
and fever of this earthly life, are yet believed to die
at last, it is not to be expected that a god who
lodges in a frail tabernacle of flesh should escape
the same fate. The danger is a formidable one; for
if the course of nature is dependent on the man-
god's life, what catastrophes may not be expected
from the gradual enfeeblement of his powers and
their final extinction in his death? There is only one
way of averting these dangers. The man-god must
be killed as soon as he shows the symptoms that
his powers are beginning to fail, and his soul must
be transferred to a vigorous successor before it has
been perilously impaired by the threatened decay."*
(p. 224-225, Italics in original)

This book is a magnificent collection of the early stories of
men and cultures, broadening and deepening the
foundations upon which we live our lives, and it resonates
with the criminal through the great richness of mythic
freedoms and the strengths of men faced with the
supernatural, which is the position without the strength
weapons bestow, of the criminal confronting the
communal world.

The rich textures, sensual framings, and personal
attraction of the individual ability to shape reality
presented by the truths of the pagan world is a large reason
for its primal attraction within the criminal world,
particularly in major carceral concentrations where
mystical physicality is of premium value in the struggle for
survival and dominance.

This field has been deeply penetrated and cultivated by
artists since before Homer and Virgil, and its more modern
fields elaborated and given even more credibility through
Jungian analysis, which itself is built upon the foundations
of myth and dreams which drove so much of the pagan
world view and its governing policy.

Being grounded (whether in reality or literally) may mean many things, but among the ancient pagan nobility, it may have meant spiritual death.

As Frazer writes:

> Montezuma, emperor of Mexico, never set foot on the ground;...For the Mikado of Japan to touch the ground with his foot was a shameful degradation...The king and queen of Tahiti might not touch the ground anywhere but within their hereditary domains.... Apparently, holiness, magical virtue, taboo, or whatever we may call that mysterious quality which is supposed to pervade sacred or tabooed persons, is conceived by the primitive as physical substance or fluid which can be drained away by contact with the earth. Hence, to preserve the charge from running to waste, the sacred or tabooed personage must be prevented from touching the ground; in electrical language he must be *insulated*. (*Ibid.* pp. 580-581, Italics in original)

From the primitive we inherited the defining of the sacred as the realm of the secret and branching from the ancient Gnostic root—Gnosticism being the first heresy, which proclaimed that the truth was reserved for the elect, remaining secret to the unworthy—came the Babel of spiritualities confusing and clouding the simple and transparent truths of Christ.

One of the most secretive of these spiritualities from the great cathedral of time is the system developed by G. I. Gurdjieff and outlined in his books, the first of which resonates under the title of *Beelzebub's Tales to His Grandson* (1973), which begins most portentously, and I remember still the wonder I experienced reading it for the first time in McNeil Island Federal Penitentiary, deeply enjoying the long elaborate sentences I have found once again in so many papal encyclicals.

Among other convictions formed in my common presence during my responsible, peculiarly composed life, there is one such also—an indisputable conviction—that always and everywhere on the earth, among people of every degree of development of understanding and of every form of manifestation of the factors which engender in their individuality all kinds of ideals, there is acquired the tendency, when beginning anything new, unfailingly to pronounce aloud or, if not aloud, at least mentally, that definitive utterance understandable to every even quite illiterate person, which in different epochs has been formulated variously and in our day is formulated in the following words: "In the name of the Father and of the Son and in the name of the Holy Ghost, Amen" (p. 3, First Book)

Thus begins an intellectual venture of profound and humorous delight that can occupy one for a very long time, even for a full lifetime, but which is built upon one principle congruent with many spiritual traditions, that of the process of self-remembering.

It is here that we call to ourselves the will to realize what it is we are doing, at all movements, for whatever purpose, and in whatever circumstances; what are we doing now?

What those who have grown to love the various messages that are embedded in the Gurdjieffian system of thinking have done is to continue what it is that Gurdjieff left them with, as he noted:

After six years of work, merciless toward myself and with almost continuously tense mentation, I yesterday at last completed the setting down on paper, in a form, I think, accessible to everybody, the first of the three series of books I had previously thought out and six years ago begun—just those three series in which I planned to actualize by means of the totality of the ideas to be developed, at first in theory and afterwards in practice, also by a means I had foreseen and prepared, three essential tasks I had set myself: namely, by means of the first series, to destroy in people everything which, in their false representations, as it were, exists in reality, or in other words" to corrode without mercy all the rubbish accumulated during the ages in human mentation"; by means of the second series, to prepare so to say "new constructional material"; and by means of the third, "to build a new world". (*Ibid.* p. 374, Third Book)

And so, the second and third series have been completed since this was written in 1950 and the system so beloved by many—including those in the criminal world attracted to the mixture of absoluteness, complete rejection of all existing and created knowledge, and the opportunity to be part of creating something entirely new—have moved on, building a better world evident best to themselves; self-involvement being the real cornerstone of the various perambulations of the New Age and the outgrowths of the first and still present heresy, Gnosticism.

Alan Watts' books continued and deepened the development of the Gnostic inspired story line elaborated into social policy driving the youth culture of the 60's, through continued explanation of why life was a game, how one could obtain the secrets about reality which were only available to the elect—thereby becoming one of the elect—and the crowning jewel of thought freeing one from the chains of the past, and, God was a myth.

In several books he worked through these ideas and in one, Watts (1972) noted:

This book explores an unrecognized but mighty taboo—our tacit conspiracy to ignore who, or what, we really are. Briefly, the thesis is that the prevalent sensation of one-self as a separate ego enclosed in a bag of skin is a hallucination which accords neither with Western science nor with the experimental philosophy-religions of the East—in particular the central and germinal Vedanta philosophy of Hinduism. This hallucination underlies the misuses of technology for the violent subjugation of man's natural environment and consequently, its eventual destruction. (p ix)

Within the criminal world, the truth of its most secret stories revolves around these set of concepts, amplified and charged with the glowing urbanities emanating from the criminal city—particularly the city at night—as the field of heroic endeavor; and breaking Watt's ideas free of their rather flowery presentation revealed a perspective resonating with its intellectual leadership.

We, all of us human beings, seek meaning in our lives—we are hard-wired to do this—and the plethora of ideas, intellectual systems, philosophies, religions and spiritual formulations that continue to be created within which we may discover it, provide something for every taste.

And long ago, at the very foundation of the world, that taste for power, darkness and the glowing embers of desire awaiting the traveler in the city at night—the criminal city first founded by Cain—was what attracted the criminal and what fulfilled the empty spaces within his world.

There may be chaos and confusion surrounding the ideas and spiritualities and that may be much of their attraction, for confusion seeks meaning as much as one who provides it controls that seeking, and Watts reminds us of that in his closing paragraph:

Now you know—even if it takes you some time to do a double-take and get the full impact. It may not be easy to recover from the many generations through which the fathers have knocked down the

84

children, like dominoes, saying, "Don't you dare think that thought! You're just a little upstart, just a creature, and you had better learn your place." On the contrary, you're IT. But perhaps the fathers were unwittingly trying to tell the children that IT plays IT cool. You don't come on (that is, on stage) like IT because you really are IT, and the point of the stage is to show on, not to show off. To come on like IT—to play at being God—is to play the Self as a role, which is just what it isn't. When IT plays, it plays at being something else." (*Ibid.* p. 143)

In a world where it often seems there is nothing that can be referenced to charity, faith or hope, the concept that God does not exist can be a seductive one, which has wrapped many deeply spiritual people who have suffered more deeply than their faith could bear, into its web.

In this bleak place, the bleakest of the prophets finds a ready home, hearth fires lit, forlornly eager faces turned to his wisdom and Friedrich Nietzsche (1954) does not disappoint:

> "Behold I teach you the overman. The overman is the meaning of the earth. Let your will say: the overman *shall be* the meaning of the earth! I beseech you, my brothers, *remain faithful to the earth*, and do not believe those who speak to you of otherwordly hopes! Poison-mixers are they, whether they know it or not. Despisers of life are they, decaying and poisoned themselves, of whom the earth is weary: so let them go.

> "Once the sin against God was the greatest sin; but God died, and these sinners died with him. To sin against the earth is now the most dreadful thing, and to esteem the entrails of the unknowable higher that the meaning of the earth." (p. 125, Italics in original)

As this pronouncement rang from the mountains, the endlessly opened Pandora's Box released the symphony of ills, which flew out and settled in the fertile plains of man's indecision and lack of faith in the message of his heart. Now, he believed, all was possible, through him alone, again. The ancient heresy once more claimed his allegiance and no better field than the dark streets of the criminal world city could be found for its bittersweet fruit.

Nietzsche's work—as does so often the work congruent with the belief that man is god rather than a child of God—informed and enhanced social developments as varied as fascism, gangsterism, socialism, uber-capitalism, atheism, relativism, and the super-individualism of the 1960's.

The ideas shaping the motivation that any individual, powerful or influential enough to do so, could reshape moral and political reality into his own image, held a seductive attraction to those unhinged from the eternal truth embedded in Catholicism and enmeshes them in a web of action leading inexorably towards spiritual destruction.

For many, the very chaos thus brought on holds an equal attraction, validating the rightness of their path as a creative and deeply inspired artist, so sadly described (in their frenzied seeking of truth in all the wrong places, leading to their eventual self-destruction) by Colin Wilson in his *Outsider* series of books.

Nietzsche, speaking through Zarathustra, writes:

> "To my final sin?" shouted Zarathustra, and he laughed angrily at his own words: "*what* was it that was saved up for me as my final sin?"

> And once more Zarathustra became absorbed in himself, and he sat down again upon the big stone and reflected. Suddenly he jumped up. "Pity! Pity for the higher man!" he cried out, and his face

changed to bronze. "Well then, *that* has had its time! My suffering and my pity for suffering—what does it matter? Am I concerned with *happiness*? I am concerned with my *work*...Thus spoke Zarathustra, and he left his cave, glowing and strong as a morning sun that comes out of dark mountains." (*Ibid.* p. 439, Italics in original)

Nietzsche, son of a Lutheran pastor who died mad, and driven by a lifelong hate of Christianity, dying himself in 1900 after years of mental illness many feel was brought on by untreated syphilis—believed to have contributed to his ideas as the advanced stages of syphilis often cause megalomania—later resented the adoption of his work by the German Reich, noting in a planned preface:

From a Draft for a Preface (Fall of 1885)

The Will To Power

A book for *thinking*, nothing else: it belongs to those to whom thinking is a *delight*, nothing else. That it is written in German is untimely, to say the least: I wish I had written it in French so that it might not appear to be a confirmation of the aspirations of the German *Reich*. The Germans of today are not thinkers any more: something else delights and impresses them. The will to power as a principle might be intelligible to them. Among Germans today the least thinking is done. But who knows? In two generations one will no longer require the sacrifice involved in any nationalistic squandering of power, and in hesitation (Formerly, I wished I had not written my *Zarathustra* in German) (*Ibid.* p. 442, Italics in original)

The first thing that struck me in reading the *Varieties of Religious Experience* by William James, was the well-evidenced good will and soundness of thinking that infuses James work, so unlike the strained neurosis characterizing so much of my reading in those years and because of that, it took some time to adjust myself to this most wondrous of thinkers.

James (1987) looks at the authors of the seminal works of Christianity, as his psychological training compels him, from a perspective that, while common now, was not so when he wrote (1901-1902), and he notes:

> Every religious phenomena has its history and its derivation from natural antecedents. What is nowadays called the higher criticism of the Bible is only a study of the Bible from this existential point of view, neglected too much by the earlier church. Under just what biographical conditions did the sacred writers bring forth their various contributions to the holy volume? And what had they exactly in their several individual minds, when they delivered their utterances? (p.13)

For the criminal struggling—though few did—with the teaching of their youth that the actions of their life were clearly wrong and would bring down upon them the severest spiritual punishment much beyond that which they now were suffering in prison; the idea that religious writing could be looked at in this relative manner, was a huge and dismissive opening for shedding that belief.

Criminal as Catholic

The ultimate source is the Catholic Church, her sacred doctrine, her social teaching and the guiding mantra I have used to access this body of holy teaching since I read it in a book by Saint Josemaria Escriva, the founder of Opus Dei, is:

With Peter, Through Mary, To Christ.

Peter is the Holy Father. Peter is all the Holy Fathers. Peter who asked to be crucified upside down so as not to imitate Christ, not the Peter who denied and ran, but the Peter who stays, Peter the rock; the Holy Father throughout the eternal history of the Church, the saintly popes whose thought and lives guide us still; and for those popes who have had their hand on the tiller of the Barque of Peter over the past several hundred years, an embracing of the works of the Angelic Doctor, the greatest theologian of the Church, Saint Thomas Aquinas.

Through Mary, whose intercessory power is unparalleled, as the Mother of God and our Mother, as the Holy See (1997) teaches us:

> **968** Her role in relation to the Church and to all humanity goes still further. "In a wholly singular way she cooperated by her obedience, faith, hope, and burning charity in the Savior's work of restoring supernatural life to souls. For this reason she is a mother to us in the order of grace."

> **969** "This motherhood of Mary in the order of grace continues uninterruptedly from the consent

89

which she loyally gave at the Annunciation and which she sustained without wavering beneath the cross, until the eternal fulfillment of all the elect. Taken up to heaven she did not lay aside this saving office but by her manifold intercession continues to bring us the gifts of eternal salvation . ... Therefore the Blessed Virgin is invoked in the Church under the titles of Advocate, Helper, Benefactress, and Mediatrix." (*Catechism* # 968- 969)

To Christ, Our Lord, who we take into our very being during Mass, whose Word will illuminate and guide our path in this life towards life eternal, and the relationship with Christ is one that must be entwined with an active interior life, as Chautard (1946) teaches us:

> *To live with oneself, within oneself;* to desire *self-control,* and not allow oneself to be dominated by exterior things; to reduce the imagination, the feelings, and even the intelligence and memory to the position of *servants of the will* and to make this will conform, without ceasing, with the will of God; all this is a program that is less and less welcome to a century of excitement that has seen the birth of a new ideal: *the love of action for action's sake....*

> This situation even called forth the celebrated letter of Leo XIII...[Apostolical Letter: *Testem Benevolentiae,* January 22, 1899, addressed to his Eminence Cardinal Gibbons, Archbishop of Baltimore, on "True and False Americanism in Religion."] in protest against the disastrous consequences of an exclusive admiration for active works.

> Priests are so anxious to avoid the *effort required to live an interior life* that they reach the point of

overlooking the value of *living with Christ, in Christ and through Christ,* and of forgetting that everything, in the plan of Redemption, is based on the *Eucharistic life* as much as it is upon the rock of Peter. (pp. 22-23, Italics in original)

The statement that we are what we become, rather than who we say we are, is so evidently self-explanatory and self-defining, that it bears no more study, but its very obviousness renders it subject to once again being explained.

The great ideas of great men and women, to have any eternal merit, must be shown to have such through their living of them and if one ends failing in virtually all aspects of greatness, then what were their ideas truly worth, except to harm those who partook of them as sustenance.

On the other hand, those great ones I later discovered, such as Thomas Aquinas, Jacques and Raissa Maritain, Mother Teresa, William F. Buckley, Alexander Solzhenitsyn, G. K. Chesterton and Hilaire Belloc, whose old age was burnished and glowing with the wisdom they had gained and shared and ratifies and concretizes their truth.

In this respect, the greatest of Catholic thinkers is surely St. Thomas Aquinas, the great Dominican, and once his work is encountered, one of the final places to look for confirmation of Catholic sacred doctrine, has been found, it is within his work.

I have been searching for a good biography of St. Thomas for some time, having exhausted the online versions of his life, and wanting a little more context. I found it in this book, and as I read the first pages which are about the period in which St. Thomas lived and his contemporaries, two of whom St. Albertus Magnus (Albert the Great) and Duns Scotus were names familiar to me from my long-ago studies in the occult, and a reminder that much of the occult is merely a perversion of authentic Catholic thought and practice; a fact really evident to me during my first experience with Latin Mass, which is the root—much perverted and demonized—of the calling down ritual used by witches.

D'Arcy (1954) writes:

> St. Thomas is no philosophic Melchisedech without ancestry, nor again the sole claimant to greatness among scholastic philosophers. His friends and contemporaries, Albert the Great and St. Bonaventure and his rival, Duns Scotus, are not dwarfed in his presence. Nevertheless tradition has rightly assigned him a certain pre-eminence, both because of the massive unity of his system and because that system reaffirms so much of the past in a measured and stately way. From the first century onwards the Christian thinkers had set to work to defend and develop the Christian teaching by adapting the current philosophic language to their creed. Their work, however, was primarily religious and apologetical and not philosophic, because they had as a principal aim to safeguard the fundamental teaching of Christianity, to state and explain what was orthodox. It mattered little what school of philosophy they adopted. The Alexandrian Fathers, for instance, differed from those of Antioch, and both were far more familiar with the technical terms of philosophy that the Western Bishops. The trouble caused by these differences in philosophical tradition is plain from the Arian, Nestorian, and other disputes. (pp. 7- 8)

For the first five or so years after my final release from prison, while I was attending college—majoring in criminal justice—and formulating the proposal for a rehabilitative program centered around college education I eventually received funding for, the reading I was doing was still connected to that which I had been reading in prison, with the very enlightening addition of criminal justice literature, which allowed me, for the first time, to begin seeing myself as others saw me.

Though the critical sociological academic perspective that treated criminals as revolutionary forerunners was very appealing to me, I knew it was largely balderdash; but it wasn't until I encountered the writings of James Q. Wilson (1975) in his book, *Thinking About Crime*, that I found writing that actually paralleled the reality about the criminal world that I had lived, criminals are criminals by choice, not because of social circumstance or psychological deficits, and these paragraphs from it capture that:

> The treatise by Sutherland and Cressey is widely viewed as the leading text on the subject of crime. Its seventh edition appeared in 1966 just after President Johnson appointed his crime commission. Professor Lloyd Ohlin, as associate director of the Commission's staff, testified to the impact of many of the book's ideas on the work of the commission.
>
> The central theme of *Principles of Criminology* is that "criminal behavior results from the same social processes as other social behavior." (Sutherland & Cressey, *Principles*, p. 59) The task of the student of crime is twofold: to show how crime varies with social structure and social processes (how it is influenced by class, neighborhood, mobility, or density) and to explain how persons are inducted into crime (by social imitation, "differential association," and attitude formation). Sutherland and Cressey review various perspectives on crime (or "schools of criminology') but fault all but the "sociological" approach. The "classical" theories of Bentham and Beccaria are rejected because their underlying psychological assumption—that individuals calculate the pains and pleasures of crime and pursue it if the latter outweigh the

former—"assumes freedom of the will in a manner which gives little or no possibility of further investigation of the causes of crime or of efforts to prevent crime." The hedonistic psychology suffers from being "individualistic, intellectualistic, and voluntaristic". (*Ibid.* p. 55) All "modern" schools of crime, Sutherland and Cressey suggest, reject this perspective and accept instead "the hypothesis of natural causation," by which they appear to mean that all other theories assume that crime is to some degree determined beyond the capacity of the individual freely, or at least easily, to resist. (pp. 42-43)

And the sociologists have not improved their approach much since then, though the latest effort to brand prisons—and thereby prisoners—as a disease, elaborately expressed by Drucker (2011) could breathe new life into the academy's meanderings.

Drucker writes:

> The new epidemic is mass incarceration—a plague of prisons. (p. 38)

> Mass incarceration easily meets the first criteria for status as an epidemic—the rapid growth of new cases (increased incidence) over a short period of time. In the past thirty-five years, the United States has increased its incarcerated population tenfold. For almost a hundred years, from 1880 to 1975, the rate of imprisonment stayed flat, averaging 100-150 individuals imprisoned for every 100,000 members of the population. Beginning in the 1970s, laws and enforcement policies were put in place that caused the rate to multiply five times over the course of thirty years, to more than 750 individuals imprisoned for every 100,000 members of the population today. This growth rate is unprecedented in our nation's history. (*Ibid.* p. 42)

While many academics consider mass incarceration as a problem—and will likely be swooning over this new narrative—criminal justice practitioners whose perspective is more balanced (for example, the criminal justice writings of James Q. Wilson) understand that the increase in prison populations is what has largely contributed, through incapacitation, the current crime rate reduction.

Rereading these books calls up my interiority from that time—an interiority I shared with so many others in prison—an interiority of diamond hardness, of dark clarity, I *knew*, and in that *knowing*, no one could reach me, surely not the soft pleas of correction—regardless of the vigor of their presentation—coming from those who did not *know*.

Knowing the truth of the Catholic Church is all you need, and though the blandishments of Marxism—or the earthly paradise—also known as liberation theology by dissenting Catholics, are very seductive, for who is not seduced by work that can change the world one sees, touches, tastes, smells, and hears; it is a mighty seduction one even those *knowing* God are prey to.

Conclusion

Virtually all of the writing on criminal justice coming from the academy is promoting the incorrect argument that crime is a result of social failing rather than the truth of Catholic teaching that it is a result of an individual decision, as the Catechism teaches us:

1868 Sin is a personal act. Moreover, we have a responsibility for the sins committed by others when *we cooperate in them*:

- by participating directly and voluntarily in them;

- by ordering, advising, praising, or approving them;

- by not disclosing or not hindering them when we have an obligation to do so;

- by protecting evil-doers.

1869 Thus sin makes men accomplices of one another and causes concupiscence, violence, and injustice to reign among them. Sins give rise to social situations and institutions that are contrary to the divine goodness. "Structures of sin" are the expression and effect of personal sins. They lead their victims to do evil in their turn. In an analogous sense, they constitute a "social sin."

Correspondingly, virtually all of the attempts to rehabilitate criminals operate from this same incorrect premise, explaining their continuous failure.

The American Church, though often forgetting this primary teaching in her pursuit of political expediency and acceptance, still remains the repository of ancient truth.

Scripture teaches us, in the complete word of revelation, that the old Covenant remains, now part of the New, and though many of the practices naturally evolve according to the signs of the times—the core dialogue remains as given—as do the immediate results of it, such as capital punishment being the just response to crimes calling out from the ground for justice.

> **1867** The catechetical tradition also recalls that there are *"sins that cry to heaven"*: the blood of Abel, (Genesis 4:10) the sin of the Sodomites, Genesis 18:20 & 19:13) the cry of the people oppressed in Egypt, (Exodus 3:7-10) the cry of the foreigner, the widow, and the orphan, (Exodus 20:20-22) injustice to the wage earner (Deuteronomy 24:14-15 & James 5:4) (*Catechism of the Catholic Church,* #1867, (1997)

The Catholic academy is a great flower in the garden of the Church, though often it produces thorns and thickets calling for radical pruning, as was the case with liberation theology, still a central praxis in the crime-as-social-failing argument and still being carried aloft as a banner of battle by many wayward elements of the Church.

The Church, as the only global institution possessing the truth of crime's source, is the only global institution able to effectively respond to the false doctrine about its cause and correspondingly, the personal rehabilitation of the criminal, the individual animating the social reality called crime.

The leadership has to come from Peter, to guide the bishops, who, on their own, tend to become fellow travelers with the secular prophet; whose current fascination with restorative justice is only the latest manifestation—parallel with liberation theology—using the language of scripture and tradition to create a new magisterium.

The last pope who spoke and wrote at a substantial level about crime was Pius XII, which, given his biography, was to be expected.

The work of past American theologians, Murray, Dulles, and one present, George Weigel—whose work on just war folds nicely into what is needed for deeper work on protecting the innocent—forms a foundation for hope.

It is so important the Church become deeply involved in the criminal rehabilitation field—there is very good work being done by the Society of Catholic Social Scientists and their two volumes & a supplement: *Encyclopedia of Catholic Social Thought, Social Science, and Social Policy* is a required reference for any Catholics working in the field—to help keep the policy and sociological conversation anchored in truth.

As it is now, the criminal justice/sociological academy is too often veering into areas of discussion so far removed from what is actually happening as a result of criminality—to the criminal and to society—that it often borders on the absurd and the recent effort to create a medical definition of prisons, Drucker (2011), noted earlier, is an example.

The only faith-based people currently involved in criminal rehabilitation at any level are the Protestants and their method of providing conversion based on emotion, never works for very long for an overwhelming majority of criminals because the rewards of the criminal life generate emotions more powerful; but the conversion by intellect— the core of the Lampstand Prison Ministry—holds, for few men will leave a hard won truth.

While in prison, I could not appreciate the intensity with which my generational cohorts outside of prison were reshaping reality; primarily through the ancient gnostic lens—though I only believed, at the time, after I was released from prison and became part of the psychedelic hippie community, that supernatural power did indeed exists—far above philosophical speculation—and it could only be accessed and wielded by adepts, which we felt we were becoming as we penetrated deeper into ourselves through the psychedelic portal.

This essential belief stayed with me in some form or another for many years, but finally began to dissipate as move evidence of the emptiness of so many of the 60's gurus became more evident. Whether reading about their foibles and follies or seeing in person their ambition addled faces radiating their lust for power and money and sex—so contrary to the proclaimed truths of 60's mysticism and enlightenment.

Becoming Catholic saved my life.

References

Aquinas, T. St. (1948). *Summa Theologica.*(Fathers of the English Dominican Province, Trans.) Notre Dame, Indiana: Christian Classics Ave Maria Press.

Baudelaire. Charles. (1991). *The flowers of evil and Paris spleen.* (W. Crosby, Trans.). Brockport, New York: BOA Editions Ltd.

Benton, W. (1960) . *Never a greater need.* New York: Alfred A. Knopf.

Benton, W. (1968). *This is my beloved.* New York: Alfred A. Knopf.

Caldwell, T. (1965). *A pillar of iron.* Garden City, New York: Doubleday & Company, Inc.

Catechism of the Catholic Church (1997).(Second Ed.) Online at http://www.vatican.va/archive/ccc_css/archive/catechism/ccc_toc.htm

Cavanaugh, R. (2012). Off the beaten path. *New Oxford Review, 79*(4), 36-38.

Charters, A. (Ed.). (1992). *The portable beat reader.* New York: Penguin Books.

Chautard, D. J-B. (1946). *The soul of the apostolate.* (T. Merton, Trans.). Trappist, Kentucky: Abbey of Gethsemani, Inc.

Cioran, E. M. (1968). *The temptation to exist.* (R. Howard, Trans.). Chicago: Quadrangle Books.

Collier, P., & Horowitz, D. (1989). *Destructive generation:*

Second thoughts about the Sixties. New York: Summit Books.

Cummins, E. (1994). *The rise and fall of California's radical prison movement.* Stanford, California: Stanford University Press.

D'Arcy, M. C. (1954). *St. Thomas Aquinas.* Westminster, Maryland: The Newman Press.

De Ropp, R. S. (1968). *The master game: Pathways to higher consciousness beyond the drug experience.* New York: Dell Publishing.

Drucker, E. (2011). *A plague of prisons: The epidemiology of mass incarceration in America.* New York: The New Press.

Eliot, T. S. (1980). *The complete poems and plays 1909-1950.* New York: Harcourt Brace.

Emerson, R. W. (1983). *Ralph Waldo Emerson: Essays & lectures.* Cambridge, England: The Library of America.

Exupery, A. d. S. (1950). *The wisdom of the sands.* (S. Gilbert, Trans.). New York: Harcourt, Brace and Company.

Flaubert, G. (2007) *Salammbo.* (Retrieved September 7, 2007 from http://www.gutenberg.org/files/1290/1290-h/1290-h.htm#2HCH0013

Frankl, Viktor E. (1959). *Man's search for meaning.* (I. Lasch, Trans.). New York: Simon & Schuster.

Frazer, J.G. (1959). *The new golden bough.* (Gaster, T. H. Ed.). New York: Criterion Books.

Genet, J. (1964). *The thief's journal.* (B. Frechtman, Trans.). New York: Grove Press.

Ginsburg, A. (1956) *Howl & Other Poems.* City Lights Books; San Francisco.

Green, M. (1991). *The dream at the end of the world: Paul Bowles and the literary renegades in Tangier.* New York: HarperCollins*Publishers.*

Gurdjieff, G. I. (1973). *Beelzebub's tales to his grandson: An objectively impartial criticism of the life of man: First, Second & Third Books.* New York: E. P. Dutton

Hesse, H. (1963). *Steppenwolf.* (B. Creighton, Trans.). New York: The Modern Library

Hesse, H. (1967). *Magister ludi.* (M. Savill, Trans.). New York: Frederick Ungar Publishing Co.

Hillman, J. (June 9, 2011). Colin Wilson at eighty: Still the outsider. *First Edition Press.* Retrieved January 30, 2012 from http://www.firsteditionpress.co.uk/?p=389

Hoffer, E. (1951). *The true believer: Thoughts on the nature of mass movements.* New York: Harper & Row.

Holy See. (1997). *Catechism of the Catholic Church: Second Edition Online Vatican* http://www.vatican.va/archive/ccc_css/archive/ca techism/ccc_toc.htm

Jackson, G. (1971). *Soledad brother: The prison letters of George Jackson.* Great Britain: World Entertainers.

James, W. (1987). *Writings 1902-1910.* New York: The Library of America

Kerouac, J. (1999). *On the road*. New York: Penguin Books.

Khayyam, Omar. (1970). *The Rubaiyat of Omar Khayyam.* (Fourth Version). (E. Fitzgerald, Trans.). Retrieved September 15, 2007 from http://classics.mit.edu//Khayyam/rubaiyat.html

Laing, R. D. (1967). *The politics of experience*. New York: Pantheon Books.

Le Bon, G. (1952). *The crowd: A study of the popular mind*. London: Ernest Benn Limited.

Mann, T. & Angell, J. W. (Ed.). (1950). *The Thomas Mann reader*. New York: Alfred A Knopf.

Maslow, A. (1965). *Eupsychian management: A journal.* Homewood, Illinois: Richard D. Irwin, Inc. and the Dorsey Press.

Maslow, A. H. (1971). *The farther reaches of human Nature*. New York: The Viking Press.

Maslow, A. (1999). *Toward a psychology of being* (3rd. Ed). New York: John Wiley & Sons, Inc.

Matthiessen, P. (1965). *At play in the fields of the Lord*. New York: Random House.

Morris, N. & Rothman, D. J. (Eds). (1995) *The Oxford history of the prison: The practice of punishment in western society*. New York: Oxford University Press.

Nietzsche, F. W. (1954). *The portable Nietzsche*. (W. Kaufmann, Trans.). New York: Penguin Books.

Pell, E. (Ed.). (1972). *Maximum security: Letters from*

California's prisons. New York: E. P. Dutton & Co., Inc.

Pope Benedict XVI. (2005). *Deus Caritas Est*. Vatican: Retrieved October 26, 2012 from http://www.vatican.va/holy_father/benedict_xvi/e ncyclicals/documents/hf_ben-xvi_enc_20051225_deus-caritas-est_en.html

Pope Paul VI (1967). *Populorum Progressio: On the development of peoples*. Retrieved October 25, 2012 from http://www.vatican.va/holy_father/paul_vi/encycl icals/documents/hf_p-vi_enc_26031967_populorum_en.html

Pope Pius V. (1982). [1566]. (McHugh, J. A. & Callan, C. J. Trans.). *Catechism of the Council of Trent for parish priests*. Rockford, Illinois: Tan Books and Publishers, Inc.

Price, L. (1959). *Stagger Lee*, Retrieved January 30, 2012 From http://www.oldielyrics.com/lyrics/lloyd_price/stag ger_lee.html

Rand, A. (1964). *The virtue of selfishness: A new concept of egoism*. New York: New American Library.

Rand, A. (1967). *Capitalism: The unknown ideal*. New York: Signet.

Rand, A. (2010). *Anthem*. Caldwell, Idaho: Caxton Press.

Ratzinger, J. Cardinal. (1997). *Salt of the earth: Christianity and the Catholic Church at the end of the millennium*. An Interview with Peter Seewald. San Francisco, Ignatius Press.

Sartre, J. P. (1963). *Saint Genet: Actor & martyr*. (B.

Frechtman, Trans.) New York: Pantheon Books.

Sciabarra, C. M. (1995). *Ayn Rand: The Russian radical.* University Park, Pennsylvania: The Pennsylvania State University Press.

Schiller. D. (2012, September 6). Resume required to join Texas prison gang. *Houston Chronicle.* Retrieved September 8, 2012 from http://www.chron.com/news/houston-texas/article/R-sum-required-to-join-Texas-prison-gang-3845881.php

Skotnicki, A. (2008). *Criminal justice and the Catholic Church.* Lanham, Maryland: Rowman & Littlefield Publishers, Inc.

Surowiecki, J. (2004). *The wisdom of crowds: Why the many are smarter that the few and how collective wisdom shapes business, economies, societies, and nations.* New York: Doubleday.

Wagoner, P. (2007). *The girl in the blue velvet band.* Retrieved September 24, 2007 from http://www.lyrics007.com/Porter%20Wagoner%20Lyrics/Girl%20In%20The%20Blue%20Velvet%20Band%20Lyrics.html

Watts, A. (1972). *The book on the taboo against knowing who you are.* New York: Vintage Books.

Watts, A. (1970). *Psychotherapy east & west.* New York: Ballantine Books.

Weigel, G. (2010). *The end and the beginning: Pope John Paul II—The victory of freedom, the last years, the legacy.* New York: Doubleday.

Wilson, C. (1956). *The outsider.* Cambridge: The Riverside Press.

Wilson, J. Q. (1975). *Thinking about crime.* (Revised Ed.). New York: Basic Books.

About the Author

David H. Lukenbill is a former criminal—
thief and robber—who has transformed his life
through education—an Associate of Arts
degree in Administration of Justice from
Sacramento City College, a Bachelor of
Science degree in Organizational Behavior
from the University of San Francisco, and a
Master of Public Administration degree from
the University of San Francisco—several years
developing, managing, and consulting with
criminal transformative organizations, and a
conversion to Catholicism.

He is married to his wife of 29 years and they
have one child. They live by the American
River in California with two cats, and all the
wild critters they can feed.

Contact information at the Lampstand
Foundation website
www.lampstandfoundation.org

Prayer for Prisoners, Pope Pius XII

O **Divine Prisoner** of the sanctuary, Who for love of us and for our salvation not only enclosed Yourself within the narrow confines of human nature and then hid Yourself under the veils of the Sacramental Species, but also continually live in the tabernacle! Hear our prayer which rises to You from within these walls and which longs to express to You our affection, our sorrow, and the great need we have of You in our tribulations - above all, in the loss of freedom which so distresses us.

For some of us, there is probably a voice in the depths of conscience which says we are not guilty; that only a tragic judicial error has led us to this prison. In this case, we will draw comfort from remembering that You, the most August of all victims, were also condemned despite Your innocence.

Or perhaps, instead, we must lower our eyes to conceal our blush of shame, and beat our breast. But, even so, we also have the remedy of throwing ourselves into Your arms, certain that You understand all errors, forgive all sins, and generously restore Your grace to him who turns to You in repentance.

And finally, there are those among us who have succumbed to sin so often through the course of our earthly lives that even the best among men mistrust us, and we ourselves hardly know how to set out on the new road of regeneration. But despite all this, in the most hidden corner of our soul a voice of trust and comfort whispers Your words, promising us the help of Your light and Your grace if we want to return to what is good.

May we, o Lord, never forget that the day of trial is an

opportune time for purifying the spirit, practicing the highest virtues, and acquiring the greatest merits. Let not our afflicted hearts be affected by that disgust which dries up everything, or by that distrust which leaves no room for brotherly sentiments and which prepared the road for bad counsel. May we always remember that, in depriving us of the freedom of our bodies, no one has been able to deprive us of freedom of the soul, which during the long hours of our solitude can rise to You to know You better and love You more each day.

Grant, o Divine Savior, help and resignation to the dear ones who mourn our absence. Grant peace and quiet to this world which has rejected us but which we love and to which we promise our co-operation as good citizens for the future.

Grant that our sorrows may be a salutary example to many souls and that they may thus be protected against the dangers of following our path. But above all, grant us the grace of believing firmly in You, of filially hoping in You, and of loving You: Who, with the Father and the Holy Spirit, live and reign forever and ever.

Amen.

O Sacred Heart of Jesus, make us love Thee more and more!

Our Lady of Hope, pray for us!

Saint Dismas, the Good Thief, pray for us!

Pius XII, April 1958

Prayer to St. Dismas

Glorious Saint Dismas, you alone of all the great Penitent Saints were directly canonized by Christ Himself; you were assured of a place in Heaven with Him "*this day*" because of the sincere confession of your sins to Him in the tribunal of Calvary and your true sorrow for them as you hung beside Him in that open confessional; you who by your love and repentance did open the Heart of Jesus in mercy and forgiveness even before the centurion's spear tore it asunder; you whose face was closer to that of Jesus in His last agony, to offer Him a word of comfort, closer even than that of His Beloved Mother, Mary; you who knew so well how to pray, teach me the words to say to Him to gain pardon and the grace of perseverance; and you who are so close to Him now in Heaven, as you were during His last moments on earth, pray to Him for me that I shall never again desert Him, but that at the close of my life I may hear from Him the words He addressed to you: "This day thou shalt be with Me in Paradise."

Amen.

Prayer to St. Michael for Protection of the Catholic Church and Her Members

℣ **Glorious St. Michael,** Guardian and Defender

of the Church of Jesus Christ, come to the assistance of the Church, against which the powers of Hell are unchained. Guard with thy special care her august visible head, and obtain for him and for us that the hour of triumph may speedily arrive.

℣ **Glorious Archangel St. Michael,** watch over

us during life, defend us against the assaults of the demon, assist us especially at the hour of death, obtain for us a favorable judgment and the happiness of beholding God face to face for endless ages.
Amen.